A
Blackburn Miscellany

Landy Publishing have also published:-

Blackburn & Darwen A Century Ago by Alan Duckworth

Bits of Old Blackburn by Chas Haworth, J.G. Shaw & Wm. Hulme
Illustrated by Charles Haworth

The Blackburn Samaritan by Trevor Moore

Blackburn's Old Inns by George Miller

Details of these and their other Lancashire books are available from:-

Landy Publishing
"Acorns"
3 Staining Rise
Staining
Blackpool FY3 OBU
Tel/Fax 0253 886103

ISBN: 1 872895 18 2

Phototypeset and printed by Galava Printing Company Limited, Nelson, Lancs.
Tel: 0282 617924

A
Blackburn Miscellany

Edited by
Bob Dobson

Landy Publishing
1993

Contents

Foreword

The idea of preparing a book of miscellaneous Blackburn historical matter came to me at the beginning of 1992. I had become aware there were a lot of interesting tales to be told, so I set about collecting some, trying to interest other people into making a contribution towards it. I set myself a deadline for *"going to the printer"*. It passed and I had achieved very little, so in January 1993 I made a resolution to pursue my aim. The result is in your hand now.

In the past two years I have enjoyed talking to and corresponding with many people, all with a love for Blackburn. I confess that my heart lies in Accrington, but I've grown to like its neighbour very much (I've long been a lover of some of Blackburn's products). I chose to work on this book because I had had some success as a publisher with Blackburn local history books, and recognised that Blackburners liked reading about their town. I've enjoyed every one of the hours I've spent in Blackburn Library, where I looked at every single item in the Local Collection. There are so many interesting aspects of Blackburn's past that, if I had been writing the book without the help of others, I would be writing till Domesday. Even now, it saddens me that I've had to miss out so much. I hope that others will decide to take up the pen to place on record some tales which shouldn't go untold.

I have to thank many people for their help towards this book — each and every one of the contributors for a start, especially Stanley Miller. I mention also Ian Sutton and his colleagues in the Library, John Lambert, Harry Hunter, Bert Hibbins, Marjorie Shorrock J.P., Jean Clegg, Tony Prince and the B.T. Archivist. I am grateful to Stephen Owens and to Mrs Monks, the District Librarian, for the use of photographs.

In the book, I have shown the name of the contributor under the title of his/her work. If there's no name shown - it's me.

Bob Johnson

August 1993

The Earliest Plan of Blackburn - 1739

Arthur Fisher

In or around 1739, one R. Lang undertook a commission to map *"the Glebe of the Rectory of Blackburn belonging to the Most Reverend the Archbishop of Canterbury"*. This plan was obtained by the Feilden family, presumably when they purchased the major part of the Rectory lands, and was discovered amongst the Feilden papers held at Blackburn Museum. A copy is held in Blackburn Library. Lang's plan provides the earliest portrait available of the market town of Blackburn, and is invaluable to the historians of the borough. It must be interpreted with some caution!

The manor of Blackburn was one of twenty eight recorded as existing in the Hundred of Blackburn at the time of the Doomsday survey, 1086. The manor had been held by Edward the Confessor prior to the Norman invasion; it contained a church. William bestowed the land on Roger de Poitu, it eventually passed to the powerful de Lacy family who built Clitheroe Castle.

The Rectors of the parish church at this time adopted the name *"de Blackburne"*. On the death of Henry de Blackburne, the land was divided between his two sons; and was to remain so divided until reunited by Feilden in 1758. One half passed into the de Hulton family, and later to the de Radcliffes and the Barton's of Smithells Hall near Bolton. In 1721, Lord Fauconberg sold his holdings to William Baldwin, Henry Feilden and William Sudell. Henry married Elizabeth Sudell, William's heiress, and bought out Baldwin. Our interest however lies with the other moiety.

The second half or moiety was purchased from Henry de Blackburne's grandson by John de Lacy, who endowed the Abbey of Stanlow on the Wirral. In 1230, de Lacy transferred to the Abbot, the patronage of the church at Blackburn, together with lands at Whalley, Blackburn and Rochdale. Income from these lands was used to build, run and maintain the Abbey. In addition, the Cistercian order had to provide a vicar for the parish church, together with his Manse and Glebe and a stipend of 40 marks per annum (£26.47). In 1296, the order migrated to Whalley with the sanction of the Bishop of Lichfield, in whose diocese it lay. For three centuries, Whalley Abbey collected the tithes of Blackburn; their tithe-barn, at the junction of Revidge Road and Duke's Brow, is shown on Lang's map.

Change came in the form of Henry's dissolution of Whalley Abbey, and seizure of the Abbey's lands: the abbot's tenants now owed their rents and tithes direct to the crown. Using funds released by the dissolution, Henry VIII created the Diocese of Chester in 1541, and in that Holy See the town now lay. Blackburn church was substantially rebuilt around the same time - this being at least the third church on the site. Why rebuilding was required, and whether the coincidence with the dissolution is fortuitous, is not clear; but this church is the one existing at the time of Lang's survey. It is shown on the plan, and existed until demolished in 1820. The tower survived until 1870.

Henry VIII evidently needed friends more than he needed half of Blackburn - for in 1547 he transferred his holding to Thomas Cranmer, Archbishop of Canterbury; from which time it has continued to be held by the Primate. Cranmer interested himself in gaining a financial reward (although he retained the privilege of appointing Blackburn's vicar). He leased the moiety to Thomas Talbot, a major local land-owner who thus became Rector of Blackburn. Effectively, Talbot gambled with the rectory - he paid a fixed sum to the Archbishop and hoped to collect in rents and tithes significantly more than he paid! He sublet to tenants, whilst possessing the right to live at Audley Hall, the seat of the Rectory.

A seventeenth century record describes Audley Hall as a substantial building of stone, timber and brick, approached by way of an avenue of trees. Talbot was a significant player in the Scottish wars, and the sight of troops moving to and from Audley became, for a time, both an entertaining and disconcerting sight for local people.

By 1616 the rental of the rectory has passed to the Fleetwood family who held it at the time of Lang's survey. In 1758, the Feilden's became rectors, reuniting the two halves of the manor. Finally in 1852, the major part of the Rectory Glebe was purchased outright by Feilden; the rest (Audley and Brookhouse) passing to the Ecclesiastical Commissioners.

As stated, Lang was commissioned to survey and record the glebe lands about 1739. He dutifully and reliably mapped the lanes and field boundaries, indicating by means of a key, the tenant of each plot. He drew symbols to represent cottages and the church, and added the name of each field. These names are of great interest to the historian.

Near to the centre of the plan is the church, near to the "T"-junction of Darwen Street and Church Street, and with the River Blakewater (the *"Black Burn"*) running close behind. The river was not the tame stream we envisage today; it could become a torrent, as in the Autumn of 1745 when twelve people were drowned in flash floods. The town lies between the river to the south and east, and the steep brow to the north.

The church shown would represent the Tudor building, c.1540. What is less distinct on Lang's plan are the cottages which almost surrounded the churchyard. These would be built mostly of wood, thatched and probably with stone or brick chimneys. It is recorded that on Christmas Day, 1642, in the height of the Civil War, Sir Gilbert Houghton chose to *"attack"* the town which was garrisoned by Parliamentary militia. The only *"casualty"* is said to have occurred when a projectile fired from the overlooking vicinity of Dukes Brow, entered the window of a churchyard cottage and burst the bottom out of a frying pan!

The Grammar School stood in the churchyard from 1568 until 1820. At this time it was a 2-storey building, timber-framed with stone footings and a slate roof. The nearby manse or vicarage would be Francis Price's rebuilding of 1680.

No Nonconformist chapel existed at this time, so dissenters were compelled to meet in their homes, or travel to Darwen, Tockholes, or Houghton Tower. The first chapel in Blackburn was for the Baptists, and was built at Islington near the Town Moor in 1764.

The cottages fronting Church Street and especially Darwen Street would generally be occupied by the well-to-do, for wide Darwen Street doubled as the Market Place, and would attract merchants, shopkeepers and traders. Lang names the tenants of these cottages, but does not signify who lived precisely where in the area. There are around 35 to 40 cottages in the centre belonging to the Rectory, some with gardens. Most are unnamed, or are simply called after the (current or former) tentant - Robert Fogg lives at *"Fogg's"*. Also mentioned are the *"Black Bull Inn"*, a *"Dog Cannel"* (a dog kennel, possibly for a pack of hounds?), and *"Fish Lane House"*, the latter the home of Henry Sudell.

At the north end of Darwen Street were the draw-well and stocks, and the stump of the old market cross, toppled during the Civil War. It was considered vital to have a route into the town, (for cattle for example) which bypassed the market and residential heart. Drovers entering from the Town Moor, could cross the river and then turn off along Back Lane, heading perhaps for Blakey Moor - the venue of the annual cattle fair. We know this thoroughfare as Mincing Lane.

West of Back Lane, Mill Lane led to the old manorial corn mill. This was operated by water taken from the Blakewater by means of a sluice and a goit, the latter is visible on the map. It is mediaeval in date, though it's origins are unrecorded, and it has been rebuilt several times. Local farmers were compelled by their leases to have their grain ground at the mill - and to pay for the privilege.

When within the streets and lanes of the town, one would be rarely out of sight of the green fields. Immediately south of the settlement, a bridge (rebuilt in 1621) crossed the burn and gave access to a common of ten acres. This land was decreed by the Duchy of Lancaster in 1618 to be *"used and employed for ever .....* *for the mustering and training of soldiers in these parts, and for the* *recreation of the inhabitants of the said town and poor thereof, as a* *gift forever"*. Forever meant until 1845 when the land was purchased by the railway company; the funds created were later used to purchase Corporation Park.

In 1764, the first Blackburn Workhouse had been built upon the Moor, and existed until the new workhouse (now Queen's Park Hospital) opened exactly a century later. Besides the river, and accessed from the bridge stood the tiny town jail. Presumably both were built upon the common land because both were thought to be of benefit to the townspeople. Some inmates might be less sure!

Southwards, across and beyond the Moor were depicted two roads - we would call them Bolton Road and Grimshaw Park, the latter lying close to the line taken by Roman legions over a millennium before. One led by Over Darwen, the other by way of Belthorne to Haslingden. The most important route however led east-west between Burnley and Preston, this forming the *"spine"* of the Hundred. The Old Road from Preston entered the town over a bridge in modern King Street, and those travelling beyond would head through the township, emerging again via Salford Bridge. From here one could proceed ahead to Rishton, Padiham or Burnley, or fork left via Little Harwood (then a separate entity) towards Whalley. The roads to Preston and Rishton were the first to be turnpiked or *"improved"*, around 1755.

The only roads out of the centre without crossing the river both involved a steep ascent. Shear Brow led northwards towards Ramsgreave; Duke's Brown towards Mellor. These, then, were the principal routes from the town; neither Preston nor Whalley New Roads existed before the 1820's. Lang also depicts a few minor roads and tracks benefitting local traffic, such as Revidge and Shadsworth Roads, and Fecitt Brow.

Before 1803, the town was governed by the County authorities and a town constable, despite the fact that it was the "capital" of the hundred. In that year twelve Police Commissioners were established by statute, with responsibility for Cleansing, Paving, Lighting and the Watch. Then a board of Improvement Commissioners was established in 1847. They took on these duties, built the new markets, and petitioned the Queen for a Charter of Incorporation. This was granted, and Blackburn Council was formed in 1851, with William Henry Hornby as the first mayor. The Town Hall opened in 1856.

Blackburn was created a Parliamentary Borough in 1832, and returned two members to parliament. Four years later, the Blackburn Poor Law Union was formed, and took on the responsibilities for relief which had previously rested with the parish.

On most roads lay cottages, farms and folds. Lang ignores whatever is not relevant to the Glebe. Bank House on Duke's Brow, for example, one of the towns principal houses, is unmarked. It presumably lay in the other half of the manor, held by Feilden *et al.* The same applies to the site long-known as Great and Little Peel. From the name, it has been suggested that this might be the site of a Norman fortified manor house, but we are unable to discern whether any building existed on the site at this era. Some of the areas, whilst not delineated or named, are nonetheless marked *"Mr. Stead's Land"* or *"Mr. John Feilding's Land"*. On the river bank, adjacent, to the church is an area marked *"Vicarage"*. Today we would recall this area as High Street (lost beneath Morrisons) and the Boulevard.

The Vicarage or *"Vicar's Glebe"* (as opposed to the Rectory Glebe), consisted of two oxgangs of land, as ordained by the Bishop of Lichfield in 1277. The Vicars of Blackburn used this area to supplement their stipend, but were rarely able to derive much income from the source. They tended to lease parcels of land, having little opportunity for farming, but tenants were slow in paying rent, and the leases in any case were only short-term. In 1795, Vicar Starkie obtained a special act of Parliament, enabling him to let his glebe on long-term leases. The timing was ideal. Industrialisation was in it's infancy, a canal was planned, and

11

entrepreneurs were seeking sites to develop the first factories. A dozen leases were completed in the first year, and soon a mill, brewery, rope-works, and streets of new houses arose to the presumed pleasure of the incumbent landlord. The map does not show the green of the Blackburn Subscription Bowling Club which stood near the vicarage from 1734 until the building of the first railway station in the early 1840's.

Other field names throw light upon the nature and use of the farmland. Near Revidge, for example, we find *Whinney Field*, and *Whinney Close*. *"Whin"* is a name for Gorse; such land would be scrubby, rough grazing. At Shadsworth, *The Mosses, Cranberry Moss and Moss End* would be poor, wet, rushy; cranberries grow well in such places.

Other land was of much higher quality. At Corporation Park we find *Nearer Marled Earth*, and *Further Marled Earth* - names relating to the widespread practice of dressing land with a mixture of lime and clay, ploughing this in to improve the quality of the soil. The higher productivity could be demonstrably successful, provided the lease was for sufficient a period to allow the would-be marler to reap his reward. Further west is a field marked *"Limefield"* from the same practice: the name persists in a terrace of houses on Preston New Road, though few of its occupants would know the origin of the name.

Each fold or farm had its croft - the small area close to the buildings were hens scratched for food, and the horse rested between duties. The *"Croft"* name appears regularly on the map. Other names depict the farming practices; *"Two Paddocks"*, *"Hay Meadows"*, *"Winter Pasture"* and *"Long Meadow"* speak for themselves. It is more difficult to discern the arable land, but many have noncomittal names - *"Five Acres"*, *"Great Hey"*, *"Smith Field"* - and there is no doubt that cornfields existed alongside the livestock. Some crops do feature: adjoining Limefields are *"Pea Field"*, and a tiny *"Wheat Croft"* - enough, perhaps, for the household's bread? At Holehouse is *"Potato Croft"*. (A croft is a small enclosed piece of land).

Writing on Lancashire agriculture in 1795, John Holt remarks dismissively that *"the north east part of the county, Blackburn, Clothero, Haslingden &c is rugged, interrupted with many rivulets, with a thin stratum of upper soil"*. He writes from the soft viewpoint of the fertile Lancashire Plain, and has little to say about these more difficult lands.

Between Shadsworth and the Knuzden Brook are several fields

12

whose names include the word *"Intack"*. These are former unproductive lands on the boundary of the town which have been *"taken-in"* for agricultural use. The locality of Intack is recognised today. Other areas of land were enclosed following the enclosure decree of 1618 mentioned above. By this decree, the Archbishop's lessee was enabled to enclose some 230 customary acres (c450 statute acres) of Revidge Moor and Coalpits Moor. Lang shows several parcels of land in outlying areas with straight edges and telling names such as *"East (or West) Moor Ground"*. Such lands appear to be marked with a capital *F, HF,* or *IF*. No key is provided, however, and the land so marked falls well short of 230 acres. Perhaps Lang omitted some land as being untenanted or still unenclosed; or the lands may have been disposed of during the intervening century.

Each agricultural tenancy has it's fold or farmhouse, and these are named in the key - *"Audley", "Oozehead", "Holehouse"* or *"Shear Brow"*. The fold was a collection of buildings, a cottage or two, barn, stable or byre, and croft. The largest holding seems to be the demesne lands at Audley, held by one Thomas Brindle. Sometimes two farms share one fold, as at Holehouse near Burnley Road. John Shrrock held a dozen of the Holehouse fields, mostly south of Burnley Road (as well as other parcels), whilst Robert Peel had a similar holding mainly north of the highway. Both also held part of the Intack. The Peels later moved to Oswaldtwistle, where they commenced careers as textile entrepreneurs and later in politics. They were destined to shape the course of history.

Few, if any, of the cottages depicted by Lang survive, but from documents and pictures and from similar buildings in other townships, it is possible to paint a word-picture of the typical yeoman's cottage of the period. It would be built of stone, have a flagged roof and one or two chimney stacks. Inside would be a large living room and a kitchen, with a couple of upstairs bedrooms. Within would definitely be a handloom (possibly two), and one or two spinning wheels; for the era of the weavers cottage with its cellar loomshop has not yet arrived. Reeds and healds vie for space with pots, pans and cakes of oatmeal; bunches of drying herbs hang from the ceiling alongside a hank of weft and half a side of bacon. Outside was the barn and a shack for the hind. The cart stood in a yard, unpaved but well trodden, and a low-walled garden of herbs, vegetables and flowers.

Most of these families would supplement a rural living with weaving; a grey cloth with linen warp and cotton weft. Yarn would be bought from the local *"putter-out"*, (working for Feilden or Sudell?), who would buy back, hopefully, the finished piece for sale in the Manchester Exchange. Lang names fields above Pemberton Clough as *"Higher White Croft and Lower White Croft"*; the name stemming from bleach-crofts where treated calico was stretched out upon the ground to bleach in the sunlight. Such fields, the ground hidden by bleaching cloth, were a common sight to all, and an irresistible temptation to the less scrupulous. The nearby field labelled *"Brick Field"* recalls another early industry - brick making.

Whitecroft stood near *Shear Bank*, another settlement comprising two farms. In this case the holdings of John Pemberton and William Howarth were so interlinked that one's fields virtually surrounded the other's. In later generations, an exchange was agreed to their mutual benefit. Two small reservoirs were built in the area in 1772, and these formed a source for the town's first piped waters supply. Today a large part of these two holdings forms Corporation Park, whilst the site of the farmsteads lies beneath Shear Bank Road. Corporation Park opened in 1857, the old reservoirs forming the park's two lakes.

Lang's map can tell us a great deal about early-Georgian Blackburn. It seems unlikely that King Street was not built upon at all, perhaps these cottages belonged to the lay part of the manor and so were omitted. By the time that Yates surveyed Lancashire in 1786, this land was built upon, as were Shear Brow and Salford.

Many of the roads shown remain as major thoroughfares today, and numerous farm and field names persist in modern usage. The local historian can enjoy many hours studying such sources, building up a view of Blackburn as it appeared in 1739.

A Stroll Round Whalley New Road Cemetery

Michael Herschell

Blackburn's town cemetery off Whalley New Road offers a haven of peacefulness within a mature and varied arboretum with magnificent views across the town. The 19 acre site was opened in 1857 at a time when a general humanitarian movement was aiming to reform and improve life in England. It belongs to the same tradition as the grander showpieces at Leeds, Highgate, Kensal Green and Brookwood. The more interesting features celebrate the Victorian attitude to life, death and the family.

The moment you enter the gates and go past the lodge, your eyes are drawn to a group of grandiloquent tombs clustered on the ridge immediately in front of you. Bear left at the war memorial and look for a cross bearing the words *"Dead he is not, but departed, for the artist never dies."* **John Francis Scott** was a Blackburn artist who died in 1903 aged 58.

Continue up the path and follow it as it curves round to a group of pinnacle style tombs. On your right is **John Thomas Baron's** partly vandalised headstone. The two side pillars have been removed but the main stone is still intact. He had many nom-de-plumes ranging from the more well known *'Jack O'Anns'* and *'Trauncer'* to *'Nora B.'*, *'Jaunty Baronius'*, *'Tummy Tulip'* and *'Bog o'Clinkums'*. He wrote over 1700 rhymes in the dialect many of which appeared in the *Blackburn Times*. Baron was a fitter and iron-turner by trade and lived much of his life in Audley. He died in 1922 aged 65 but will be remembered for the sympathy he showed for the under-dog and for his homely philosophy.

Almost next door to Baron's grave is the pinnacle tomb belonging to the Sharples family. **James Sharples** was a painter, engraver and blacksmith whose chief claim to fame is his picture *'The Forge'* now hanging above the stairs of Blackburn Museum. Although dulled by age it is still possible to appreciate the beauty of line and of light and shade that characterise his work. He is mentioned in Samuel Smiles' book *'Self-Help'* which emphasises the way he was able to find time for his art despite working long hours in the foundry. Even after his success with *'The Forge'* he continued

15

to work up to fourteen hours a day at Yate's Forge in Blackburn virtually until his death in 1983.

A brief detour across the grassy circle that was once the Anglican chapel and up the path to the top will bring you to **Fred Kempster's** grave. His stone states that he was *'The British Giant'* and herein lies his fame. Originally from Landermere in Essex, Fred Kempster grew at the rate of four inches a year to reach the grand height of eight foot four. Statistically, he broke many records. He weighed 27 stone and had a reach of thirteen feet, enabling him to light a cigarette from a street gas lamp. His hand could stretch to two octaves on the piano; an old penny (similar in diameter to a 50p piece) would go through his gold ring; his normal breakfast consisted of four loaves of bread and six eggs. More macabre are the figures relating to his death. He became ill whilst appearing in a one-man show in a draughty shop in Victoria Street. Once at Queen's Park Military Hospital, he required a row of three beds to lie upon. He finally died of pneumonia on April 15th 1918. His coffin was over nine feet long; ten tons of earth were excavated from his grave and fourteen men were needed to lower his coffin into it.

Take the right hand path down towards the Roman Catholic chapel and then walk along the lower path. **William Billington's** (born April 3rd 1827) chest tomb is easily distinguishable on the right hand side of the path. In particular, look out for the Karl Marx style face of Billington carved at each end of the chest. Like *Jack o'Ann's*, he was a poet of Lancashire dialect - *'Sheen and Shade'* (1861) and *'Lancashire Songs'* (1883). Originally from Samlesbury he worked as a doffer, a stripper and grinder and finally as a weaver in various mills in the town. His first poetic contribution was to the *Blackburn Standard* in 1850 and he wrote regularly in the *Blackburn Times* from 1855. He died, aged 57, in 1884.

The final gravestone is nearby but has to be searched for. The memorial to **James Pitt VC** is relatively new, it being erected in black stone in 1970.

Along with Private Robert Scott of Haslingden, Private James Pitt defended the slopes of the hill below Caesar's Camp during the Siege of Ladysmith (the Boer War 1900). They were the only two men left out of the sixteen men in 'D' Company, Manchester Regiment and Pitts continued fighting alone, even after Scott was wounded, until relieved by the Rifle Brigade. Both men received the Victoria Cross.

James Pitt was born on 26th February 1877 and lived at 33 Barton Street. After the Boer War, he married and settled in Blackburn though he did go to fight in the First World War. He died on 18th February 1955 and is remembered both here and, with Blackburn's three other VC's, on a special tablet in the entrance to the old Town Hall.

Elizabeth Ann Lewis:
"An exceptional woman"
Helen Wood

On Wednesday the 19th March 1924, an impressive funeral procession, of almost royal proportions, passed along the silent streets of Blackburn. Thousands lined the route from the chapel to the cemetery, people of all sorts; including workers from the neighbouring mills, while many of the public houses drew their blinds and closed their doors in tribute as the cortege passed. This was evidently the funeral of some eminent person, much respected and deeply mourned, but had some chance stranger asked for more information, he would have learned what a loss the town had suffered in the death of their own *"Queen of Temperance"*, known far and wide with every justification, as *"The Drunkards' Friend"*. His informant might have gone on to describe Mrs. Lewis's lying in state in her own Mission Hall for the twentyfour hours before the funeral, in an open coffin, robed in her customary black, on a platform swathed in purple and white. Thousands came to say farewell; rich folk and poor folk, men in formal suits and men in caps and mufflers; ladies in their furs along with girls in clogs and shawls, all queueing patiently to do honour to this much-loved lady.

In the avalanche of tributes to the valuable work of Elizabeth Lewis which followed her death, speakers and writers stressed how unusual it had seemed, at the time, for a woman to begin such an undertaking as her Mission, and to achieve so much. It was felt to be an appropriate recognition of the strides since taken by women in many areas of public life over the years, not least in the Women's Temperance Movement, that the Guard of Honour at the lying in state, and accompanying the hearse on its slow journey to the cemetery, should be provided solely by women, many of them Mrs. Lewis's Band of Hope girls.

By the 1920's some portion of the shackles restricting women had been shaken off, but few individuals could show such astonishing progress as the shy Shropshire girl, who had come to Blackburn as a twenty year-old bride 56 years earlier (1868). The Temperance principles in which she had been reared by devoted parents were shared by her cousin, Thomas Lewis, who took her from her country home to industrial Lancashire, to work by his side in his newly opened coach building enterprise.

Lizzie, as she was always known, could scarcely have foreseen, as she devoted herself to her duties as wife and mother, the successful career as Temperance worker, speaker and organizer, which came to her unsought, and which was to make her a major national figure in her chosen field.

In vivid contrast to the often hectic activity of the later years, her early days in Blackburn were quiet and uneventful. Like many another 'foreigner' Lizzie had much to learn in order to take her place, as she earnestly wished, as a capable, methodical Lancashire housewife, like those she saw around her. Young and nervous, but anxious to do well, she never forgot the warm-hearted, helpful neighbour who took time to initiate her into the mysteries of donkey-stoning doorsteps, a local domestic art-form hitherto unknown to her. The young bride could appreciate the importance of this external evidence of housewifely pride and self-respect, but without expert tuition, the skill needed to achieve the desired effect was not easy to acquire. All her life Mrs. Lewis liked to make a good job of whatever task she undertook. Stoning doorsteps and windowsills was no exception.

This characteristic came into play as the young couple worked together to build up Thomas's business. To help with the upholstery side of the carriage trade. Lizzie worked hard to master the different processes. Her early education, concentrating on her musical talents, (she was an accomplished pianist), had pointed her in an entirely different direction, but now that love and marriage had brought her to Blackburn, she set herself to play her part equally in the home and in the workshop. She and Thomas, still resolute in their Temperance convictions attended the Good Templars' meetings regularly, but she, never one to push herself forward, could never bring herself to speak in public at this stage. She was still far too shy to do more than occasionally oblige on the piano. It was the British Women's Temperance Association which she and her mother joined in 1882, which gradually drew her on to develop organizational and other skills which had lain dormant until the pressing needs of the hour called them forth.

Whether Blackburn deserved the discreditable title of 'the most beery town in England', or not; at this period, certainly, like many industrial towns, it offered plenty of scope for people like Mrs Lewis and her helpers. There was a liquor license of some kind for every 34 houses in the town, and drunkenness, with its attendant poverty and domestic miseries, was rife. To face this problem, Elizabeth realized that in spite of her fears and intense nervousness, she must become a public figure. She did become a reasonably competent speaker, welcomed everywhere for her earnestness and warmth of personality, but it was her ability to communicate face to face which was her greatest strength. This would explain how she was able to make so many *"converts"*, and to keep so many of them loyal to their pledges for life.

Her first experience in helping at a *"Blue Ribbon"* meeting, was almost a disaster. Her nerve completely failed as she attempted to speak from the platform. It was as much a surprise to herself as to her colleagues, that she took so readily to *"taking pledges"* from the audience. This strengthened her resolve to devote herself personally to tackling the problem of heavy drinking. From this grew the Mission, always non-denominational and non-political. She was aided by many loyal helpers, but took charge of the enterprise herself, *"unhampered"*, as she put it, *"by a Committee"*. This was her own creation, and she stamped her personality on it as it grew and developed. Thomas backed her up every inch of the way, even to incorporating a beautiful new meeting hall into his new business premises in St. Peter Street. Even the withdrawal of repair work by a brewery, because of Mrs. Lewis's campaign did not deter him; husband and wife were equally committed.

During the years when she travelled widely to fulfil speaking engagements all over the country, an easily recognizable figure with her smiling face and Victorian ringlets, Lees Hall and Blackburn always remained the central core of her interest. She would travel all night in order to get back home. The work of The Hall reflected the personality of its founder, a warm and welcoming venue for Penny Readings, Musical Evenings, and other entertainments, designed to counteract the *"Free and Easies"* put on by the public houses. A popular element of the Lees Hall evenings was the *"Before and After"* experiences of the *"converts"*, related by themselves with as much drama and pathos as they could put into them. Colourful characters like *"Owd Dash the Navvy"* were particularly appreciated. Navvies had a long run of popularity as working-class heroes.

Mrs. Lewis considered home-visiting to be an essential part of her work. Although she never became a really outstanding speaker, she could bring the house down with her account of the archetypal slum home of a drunken couple, furnished with the usual three orange boxes and a heap of rags. This story finished up with the triumphant retrieval from the Workhouse of *both* aged mothers, an achievement recognized in fact and fiction alike, as the epitome of respectability and rehabilitation. She is known to have disarmed more than one drunken harridan, attempting to shout her down at a meeting, using only sympathetic words and a sisterly embrace. She thought nothing of keeping one of her *"waverers"* comapny in his humble home until the pubs closed, and turning up next morning at 6 a.m. to make sure he got to work safely. Even the good and the great were not beneath her notice if she felt she might do them some good. For example she is known to have sought an interview with Gladstone, and to have tried to convert Winston Churchill to Total Abstinence.

In spite of her popularity all over Britain and beyond, and the success of her work, Elizabeth's life-work was by no means always marked by sunshine. Certain bigoted religious factions diapproved of her non-sectarian approach, others hinted darkly that *"nobody ever did owt for nowt"*, and wondered if the Mission finances would stand being looked into. Members of the licensed trade, some of whom had never ceased to snipe at her, spread scandalous rumours about her personal behaviour. She was completely vindicated in court, and was drawn home in triumph by a team of her reformed drinkers.

"A natural dynamo", *"a great-souled woman"*, *"a spreader of happiness"*, she succeeded in helping to make Blackburn a more sober and pleasant place. Perhaps the secret of that success lay in the words of one tribute after her funeral;

"She believed in the innate goodness of people".

Wainwright's Blackburn
Ken Fields

I often wonder how many fell-walkers, who, having scaled the lofty heights of Lakeland's Helvellyn and Scafell Pike, have then been inspired to make a pilgrimage to Blackburn. For here they surely ought to come to discover the hometown of England's most famous walker and mountain writer, Alfred Wainwright. This remarkable man, whose classic mountain guide books have become the bible of all who walk in the Lake District, spent the first 34 years of his life here. Although there have been changes since the pre-war days of his youth, many of the sites he knew so well remain and a trail is being created for those who wish to walk in his footsteps.

The cosy terraced house in which he was born on the 17th January 1907, has miraculously escaped the path of the bulldozer. Lying on the Accrington road, No. 331, Audley Range, is now the home of Kathleen Godfrey who is proud to live in *'a bit of Blackburn's history'*. In the year following his death, 1992, the Civic Society was quick to remember him by erecting a blue plaque on the wall of his childhood home. What A.W., (as he liked to be known), would have made of all this fuss is open to speculation, but those who knew him best feel that inwardly, at least, he would be well pleased.

His early life in Edwardian Blackburn was tough, but as he later recalled, this was not the whole story. People also *"had pride, courage, character, honesty and an observance of moral standards not seen today"*. The Wainwright family had originated from Penistone in Yorkshire, but A.W.'s father who was a travelling stone-mason, settled in Blackburn, His mother, with four children and her husband to feed, bore the main burden of their poverty which was commonplace at this period. *"I used to wake in the middle of the night and I could hear the mangle going in the kitchen. To make ends meet she had to take in washing"*, A.W. remembered.

His urge to explore the hills came at an early age but *"none of my pals would come with me"*. So alone and not yet seven, with a jam-butty in his pocket, he took his first solitary walk to the top of local beauty spot, Darwen Tower. This round trip of 12 miles was to begin his love-affair with wild, unspoilt landscape, which was destined to last throughout his life. His artistic skill was also becoming apparent at this period, for he would spend much of his free time painstakingly copying the cartoon characters from his comics.

Showing above-average intelligence he was saved the fate of a dead-end job in a mill at the age of 12, by earning a further year of education. At 13 he started as an office boy in the Borough Engineer's Office at Blackburn Town Hall and later transferred to the Treasurer's Department. With pride he ran all the way home to give his mother his first weekly wage of 15 shillings.

In 1930, accompanied by a cousin from Yorkshire, he took his first holiday in the Lake District, which was eventually to change his life. Here he discovered a magical, enchanted landscape that was his idea of heaven. The pair conquered their first Lakeland summit, Frostwick, they went on with their adventure by climbing many other peaks including a traverse of Striding Edge, then only with reluctance did he return to his work in Blackburn. However, there were the twin compensations of watching the Rovers on Saturday (A.W. was a founder member of the Supporter's Club) followed by a meal of fish and chips, which remained his favourite dish to the end of his life.

The next decade saw the death of his father, his marriage and the birth of his son. But the desire to explore the northern hills remained as strong as ever. At every opportunity he would explore the local moorland, walk over the Yorkshire Dales, or return to his beloved Lakeland. Then in 1941 he heard of a vacancy in the Council Treasurer's Office at Kendal. Although it meant a salary reduction it also meant he could live close to the mountains, so he quickly applied for the position and was successful.

He was now able to spend each weekend exploring every craggy summit and every hidden valley in Lakeland. Within ten years he had acquired an unsurpassed knowledge of the area, which he was intent on passing on to others in the form of a guide book. He wrestled with the problem of how best to convey the mountainous terrain in print, then he came up with a unique solution. Using his natural artistic skill together with his beautiful handwriting, perfected over many years of writing out ledgers, he completed his first volume by hand. Filled with line drawings, maps and personal anecdotes it was published by a local printer at Kendal in 1954.

His book, which covered the Eastern Fells, was an instant success, so he continued his labour of love covering the whole Lake District in seven volumes. These proved so popular that their publication was taken over by the Westmorland Gazette. By this time he had been appointed as the Treasurer for Kendal Council, so his writing continued as a part time activity. He had never learnt how to drive so he was forced to use irregular local bus services to reach many isolated places. Only after his second marriage to Betty, who could drive, did he enjoy the luxury of a car. He then went on to write guide books to other areas, including Scotland and the Yorkshire Dales. At the time of his death he had written over fifty volumes and sold over a million copies, and had gained national fame by reluctantly appearing in a series of TV films.

One of A.W.'s nephews, Jack Fish, who still lives in Blackburn, remembers with affection the uncle who took him picnicking on sunny days to Darwen Tower. A.W. was over six feet tall and at this time *"his hair was ginger but darkened by using Brilliantine, which was the fashion in the thirties,"* Jack recalls. *"He returned to Blackburn at least three times each year to watch the Rovers, and he would have been very proud of their recent success in the Premier League."* Sadly, it seems that none of A.W.'s family have inherited his passion for walking, although a little of his artistic talent is apparent in some relatives.

Alfred Wainwright was an independent Blackburnian who was intensely proud of his northern roots. His unique literary and artistic skill was the vehicle which allowed him to convey the beauty of the Lakeland mountains and this to him was reward enough. Until the latter end of his life he managed to successfully maintain his privacy, ignoring the fame which his books brought to him and when he died in 1991 he left most of his royalties to an animal charity. However, his greatest epitaph will lie in the future generations who through his books will continue to discover the joy of fell-walking.

One of Blackburn's Pioneering Photographers

Andrew Kit

Richard Wolstenholme took up the art of photography at the age of 22. He was born on the 6th March 1842 in Rhodes, near Middleton on the outskirts of Manchester. At the age of 10 he left school and went to work at the Messrs. Salis, Schkabe & Co. where his father was also employed. He worked 6 a.m. to 8 p.m. and sometimes to 10 p.m. for the 2/6 a week wage. Later he was moved to the machine room and then promoted to the drawing shop where he undertook a 7 year apprenticeship as a sketch maker, producing patterns to be engraved on the copper plates which were printed onto calico. A few months after completing his apprenticeship in 1864 a fellow apprentice was selling his photographic equipment. From this point his career as a photographer began. The original set-up which he bought consisted of a wooden box camera with a quarter plate French lens, bottles of silver nitrate, collodion, iron protosulphate, potassium cyanide and a few quarter plate glass photographic plates and frames. Within a year of buying this equipment and pursuing his new-found hobby he spent almost £70.

A rabbit hutch, a rain tub and other inanimate objects where the first subjects for his camera but through perseverance and dedicated hard work he moved on to his patient friends. With his brother, who assisted him with his pursuits, he constructed a canvas studio to help with the developing process. With the co-operation of Mr. Wolstenholme's boss, and the updating of his equipment, he and his brother were given time off to photograph customers. It was through the boss' generosity that the brothers realised the potential to be made through photography and set up business. Photography was then no easy achievement. Hard work as well as a knowledge of chemistry was required as some of the ingredients required careful handling. The amount of equipment needed was vast even for a field trip. On one occasion Mr. Wolstenholme took a *portable* outfit on a trip to Buxton. The outfit consisted of a 12 x 10 landscape camera and lens, a box of plates with a matching empty box to carry the exposed plates, a sterilizing bath, a large bottle of treacle syrup to keep the plates wet until the image was fixed back home. This was all packed into a 3ft. square wooden box which in total weighed over 112 lbs and was carried for 30 miles.

It was in October 1873 when Mr. Wolstenholme set up a photographic business in Blackburn while his brother continued to run their established Blackpool branch. He opened at 59 Higher Eanam but later moved to a town centre location at 4 Preston New Road where he built his studio at the rear. There he continued until retiring in 1889. Photography was still his passion and he became the inaugural president of the Blackburn & District Photographic Society in 1901. The society's aim was to assist the amateur in all aspects of photography. For the annual fee of 5s. members were given lectures (some of which were given by Mr. Wolstenholme) and assistance. Occasionally there were organised field trips where members were given on-the-spot advice but the advancement in photography had now made it a point and shoot affair. He held the post for two years then continued on the committee. His wealth of experience lead him to become a member of lecturing staff of the Lancashire & Cheshire Photographic Union. During his career as a professional he took over 50,000 portraits.

A Chat Wi' Owd Bert Hibbins

Nick Howorth

In the *Blackburn Times* of 4th April 1936 appeared a report that Mr Herbert Hibbins of 137 Dukes Brow had retired from the Post Office after working for 45 years and was being presented with the Imperial Service Medal by the Blackburn postmaster, Mr C. Harvey. Mr Hibbins had worked under seven Postmasters and had walked a quarter of a million miles along Blackburn streets delivering letters. His son, also Bert, is (1993) now 82 years young, and has lived all his life on Dukes Brow, excepting for wartime service. He had 3 brothers and 3 sisters. Bert's working life was spent as a driver for Whalley's of Ainsworth Street (and later Weir Street), wholesale grocers, delivering to corner shops throughout East Lancashire. The firm closed when Bert had been there for 47 years. Not being ready for retirement, Bert got himself a job with Bullock's china shop in Mill Lane, then one as a caretaker in King George's Hall. The pension and bus pass didn't mean retirement though, as he then became a caretaker for a solicitor for another nine years. Let's engage in conversation over a pint in The Quarryman's ... (That's him sat in t'corner wi' t'cap on ...)

Nick: "Well, Bert, you've lived on Dukes Brow for more than 80 years, and you know more about this area than anyone I've ever met."

Bert: "I've always been interested in Blackburn's history. I got it from my father Herbert who came here aged 5 in 1881. He was a postman for 47 years and he knew every street in Blackburn. They gave him the Imperial Services Medal when he retired."

Nick: "We know that Dukes Brow is one of the oldest streets in Blackburn. An old road to Preston came up from Snig Brook, past Bank House at the bottom end of Dukes Brow. This is Blackburn's oldest house."

Bert: "Yes, I have a distant connection with Bank House. I was born at 122 Dukes Brow which was previously owned by Mr Jack Hand. His sister married a Mr Wilson who owned Bank House. Their son and daughters still live there."

Nick: "That part of Dukes Brow where you were born has a special name. Can you tell me about it?"

Bert: "The row of houses backing onto Wagtail Quarry up Leopold Road, just higher up the Brow than the Quarryman's was known as "Wagtail", and anyone living there was a "Wagtailer". Mr Peter Evans of 129 Dukes Brow was known as "the mayor of Wagtail". His daughter was my Godmother. On special occasions he would ride on a white horse over to "Pinchem" on Revidge Road, which is now called the West View Hotel. The folk who lived there in the adjacent handloom weavers cottages also used to elect a mayor who would ride over to the Quarryman's Arms for an exchange visit."

Nick: "I wonder whether any other parts of Blackburn elected their own mayor? I think your mayor of Wagtail was connected with Mr Jack Smith who was the first owner of Wagtail Quarry and was elected Mayor of Blackburn in 1867. He also used to live at Bank House. There are some funny stories about him in Miller's "Bygone Blackburn". You once told me that West View Place, around the corner from the West View Hotel (Pinchem to you) was called "Double Street", and Mile End Row was called "Treacle Row". My theory is that "Double Street" referred to both what is now West View Place and an older back street or farm track that ran up from St. Silas's Road, past the almshouses, and up the hill to the old farm behind "Pinchem". A small part of the ruins of the farmhouse is still preserved behind the West View Hotel. I also think that "Treacle Row" led to a treacle or holy well in the field at the end of the street."

Bert: "Do you know anything about the handloom weavers colony on West View Place and Mile End Row?"

Nick: "Well, Brian Lewis says the houses were built in 1818-1820 in his book "Life in a cotton town: Blackburn 1818-1848". At that time most of the weaving around Blackburn was still home-based. Access to the West End colony would have been greatly improved when the Blackburn to Preston turnpike (which we call Preston New Road) was opened in 1826. This new turnpike opened up a "green belt" in which some of Blackburn's wealthy families built themselves big houses near here such as Billinge Scarr and Beardwood Hall."

Bert: "Isn't it curious that whilst everyone knows about East Lancs, very few people know that Blackburn Rovers' first ground was near here?"

Nick: "I have always followed the Rovers. My grandfather used to live at 126 Nuttall Street across the road from the grandstand at Ewood Park. I heard tell that the Rovers used to play near Fox

Delph at Limefield."

Bert: "No, it was nearer here than that. It was called *"the Leamington Ground"*, and was situated where Leamington Road Baptist Church now stands. Wellfield Road, off Granville Road, between the Rovers' ground and Dukes Brow, was called *"Rover Street"*.

Nick: "Have you ever noticed how many houses around the West End of town were built in the 1860s? I understood that was because of the American civil war."

Bert: "When the union forces blockaded the confederate cotton ports it resulted in massive unemployment in the Lancashire cotton industry. Under the Public Works Act many out of work weavers had to work as labourers on projects like making the carriage drive through the Corporation Park up to Revidge Road. I expect all the house building done at that time using local stone used the same cheap labour."

Nick: "My own cottage on Revidge is a two-up, two-downer, dating from 1864. It still has a stone-flagged floor and a big open hearth with a dog grate. Many of the local pubs used to have a stone-flagged entrance passage, so that workmen with dirty clogs could be served through a hatch. *"The Dog Inn"*, *"The West View"*, and *"The Bay Horse"* on the Yellow Hills were like that in the 1940s. As the West End grew in prosperity there must have been quite a few well-known people living locally."

Bert: "The most famous person from these parts was Miss Kathleen Ferrier who lived until she was 22 years old at 57 Lynwood Road, just around the corner from here. When we were young she and I were in the same gang of kids who used to play together in Higher Bank Street. Many years after she died the Council put up a plaque outside the house. Another famous person who also deserves to have a blue plaque put up was Mr Philip Snowden who used to live at 2 Leopold Road, just across the road from here. He was the son of a weaver and was M.P. for Blackburn from 1906-1918 when he lost his seat because of his pacifist views."

Nick: "Mr Snowden was Chancellor of the Exchequer in both of Ramsay MacDonald's two labour governments as well as his first national government, whilst in the second national government he was Lord Privy Seal. Alan Taylor wrote that Snowden was a social reformer who nevertheless believed in a balanced budget. Any chancellor who said that today would be told he was to the right of Genghis Khan."

Bert: "Aye; more's the pity. Then there as a lady author called

The Quarryman's Arms, Dukes Brow drawn by Paul Snell of Bartle

Miss Dorothy Whipple who lived at 12 Merlin Road. I used to deliver the Northern Daily Telegraph there when I was 12 years old. Then, finally, another person who was very important in his day was Sir John Rutherford who lived in a big house on Beardwood Brow. He was in the brewing trade."

Nick: "A trade directory for Blackburn in 1889 says that at that time there were three breweries in the town: Dutton's Salford Brewery, Thwaite's Eanam Brewery, and Henry Shaw's Salford New Brewery. John Rutherford was Mayor of Blackburn in 1889 and was one of the two chief executives, as we call them today, at Shaw's brewery. He must have got his knighthood later on for *"political services"."*

Bert: "It must have been a tight fit, getting two big breweries in on Salford."

Nick: "Ah well, Salford has shrunk over the years, and Eanam has grown! If you look at an early map, like Gillie's of 1822, in those days Salford ran up from Penny Street to Syke Street, whilst Eanam was a short piece from the canal to Thwaite's brewery. My dad was a Bert like yourself and was the clerk of works at Dutton's, Shaw's was bought out by Dutton's."

Bert: "Sir John had three houses built on Revidge Road, 108, 110, and 112, for his chauffeur Mr Green, his valet Mr Read, and his business secretary Mr Sweeting."

Nick: "I knew Miss Stella Read, who would have been the daughter of Sir John's valet. She taught me at St. Silas's Church Sunday School nearly 50 years ago."

Bert's drinking career covers sixty years so far. He has seen prices rise from 5d a pint to today's price, which is sixty times as much. Bert mentioned *"The Yellow Hills"*, this is the local name for the fields to the west of Billinge Woods, which is now a public park. The name comes from the gorse bushes growing wild there. He also mentioned *"The Bay Horse"*, this has changed its named to *"The Clog and Billycock"*.

Thomas Swinburne of Blackburn, Railway Pioneer

On 8th January 1881, Thomas Swinburne died at his home in Shear Brow aged 68 years. He came from a family who had been associated with railways from their very earliest days and he himself was recruited by George Stephenson in the North-East to work on track-laying on Lancashire's first railway, between Bolton and Leigh, when 16 years old.

Moving to lay track on the tram road between Walton Summit and Preston, he introduced his ideas to that line, particularly his methods of *"catch points"* to prevent trucks running backwards if a chain broke.

In 1846, after 4 years as an inspector on the Bolton, Chorley & Preston Railway, he moved to the Lancashire & Yorkshire (the L & Y) Railway, responsible for track in the Farington area. He later worked on the Fleetwood line and near Huddersfield. After 18 months absence, the East Lancashire directors asked him to return and gave him charge of the permanent way. On amalgamation with the L & Y, he remained at Blackburn with the same responsibilities.

In his working life, although he held no patents, Swinburne introduced many improvements connected with points and signals. These lead to greater safety and many are still in use today.

Although he travelled over a million miles by railway, he was involved in only one accident - at Horwich in 1840, whilst in a seat on the outside of a carriage he was struck by the spur of a bridge when travelling at 8-10mph.

In such esteem was Swinburne held that a stone carving of his head was erected at a station near Huddersfield, and this was later transferred to the National Railway Museum, York.

Thomas Swinburne was a benefactor of Hoghton Church, where he lies. He contributed heavily towards the cost of the church organ in 1869.

Chad Varah: a Blackburn Samaritan

Edward Chad Varah came to Blackburn in 1942 aged 30 years from a church in Barrow in Furness to be the vicar of Holy Trinity Church. He had a reputation for inter-demoninational Christian work and was a Rotarian.

Popular with his parishioners, he had a huge appetite for work. In addition to his local pastoral work, he was editor of the National Church's magazine *"The Crosier"*, and lectured on subjects ranging from Russian language to astromony, theology to English literature. He could properly be likened to Rev Grosart, mentioned elsewhere in this book. In later years he would become a leading figure in the editing of that popular boys' comic *"The Eagle"*.

Three sons and a daughter were born to Mr & Mrs Varah during their seven years at Holy Trinity, and a happy family life contributed to his well-being.

Sometime during the war, the Roman Catholic wife of one of Chad's parishioners ran off to Ireland with their baby son. One of Chad's churchwardens, related to the distraught husband, approached Chad for help. It was believed she had gone to Southern Ireland to her father. She had been corresponding with a nun who had told her she had committed a mortal sin by marrying a Protestant and allowing their child to be christened a Protestant. She would go to Hell if she didn't leave her husband.

Secretly, Chad went to Ireland and took part in a plan to capture the child. The story would make a good film. It involves Chad being approached by a prostitute, and a taxi driver tipping off the police, who arrested Chad and charged him with child stealing. Released on bail, he was returned to Blackburn, where he was treated as a front-page hero. A Defence Fund was set up. He was subsequently found *"Not Guilty"* of stealing, but guilty of common assault. The sentence was six months imprisonment unless Chad consented to be bound over for good behaviour for a year. The court awarded custody of the boy, Kevin, and of an unborn child, to the Blackburn father. A story with an almost happy ending.

Chad left Blackburn in 1947 for a Battersea parish to concentrate on his plan for lay evangelism in the Church, which he called *"Operation Snowball"*. He had the feeling that he knew how to make the pastoral and evangelical work of the church more effective and economical, and he felt it was his duty to try out his plans. If London was prepared for a bold experiment, and Blackburn wasn't, his choice was obvious.

To mark his leaving, local change ringers rang a peal of *"Bob Major"*, with 5040 changes in 2 hours 50 minutes. Chad Varah was yet to ring his personal big bell.

A local journalist recognised that the town was *"losing a remarkable man who had not spared himself in utilising his intellectual attainments"*. For his part, Chad spoke of the friendliness, neighbourliness and generosity of the ordinary Blackburn citizen. He went on to comment that he felt the religious life of the country was hampered by the almost fanatical rivalry between R.C.'s and Protestants.

Chad Varah achieved his ambition, or one of them, in 1953 when the first *"Samaritans"* office opened in London. This human dynamo with Blackburn connections is recognised as the founder of that fine organisation of anonymous Christians who help the helpless. There is a group of Samaritans in Blackburn. I hope they are aware of Blackburn's contribution to the movement. Long may they prosper whilst a need for them exists.

A Modern-times Captain of Industry — Stanley Shorrock

One is tempted to believe that all of Blackburn's entrepreneurs were Victorians. Far from it. Such a person, Stanley Shorrock, was born in the town on 14th June 1926 and through his own inventiveness and drive went on to become a major employer, and the first to occupy a site on the town's first specially-created industrial estate, Shadsworth.

Young Stanley studied at Blackburn Technical College, but his education was cut short by the asthma which undoubtedly was affected by Blackburn's polluted air. He became a marine engineer in the Royal Navy, using his inventive mind to develop a noise-reducing device to deaden the noise of motor torpedo boats. Ill-health forced him out of the Navy and back to Blackburn to work on marine boilers. After a short spell out of town, he returned for good in 1950 as chief engineer employed by Frank Mercer at Pioneer Mill. There were produced woven goods for customers such as Marks & Spencer, and there Stanley collaborated with the boss' son, Brian Mercer, who in later years founded the Netlon Corporation - he's another Blackburn captain of industry.

Stanley had inventiveness and vision, but needed to finance his business ideas. At home, he used his mother's sewing machine to experiment with his ideas.

In 1955, Stanley joined Brian Mercer, who had formed Tufting Machine Company, making machines they had invented and patented, and which could do the job far faster than any competitor's machines. Amongst their customers was Cyril Lord, the post-war carpet king. Tufted carpet was a boon to families who didn't want their floors covered with austeer *"oil cloth"* (linoleum) yet couldn't afford traditional woollen carpet. In a short space of time, 99% of all tufting machines existing in the world were made post-war in Blackburn. At this time, Stanley spoke of his wish that the name *"Blackburn"* would become synonymous with quality carpet just as *"Wilton"* and *"Axminster"* were.

After a few years the Company was sold out to the Singer Cobble Company, who sought to alleviate the competition. Stanley sought other avenues for his busy mind, and in 1961 founded Shorrock Developments in an office above a dentist's surgery in Preston New Road. The work done there was in the design and production of security and radio communications, especially for police and aviation customers. Soon the firm was expanding and in need of the factory space which was available at Shadsworth. Who designed the factory ? - Stanley Shorrock.

Although he had little time for anything except his business and was always conscious of the need to provide wages for his employees, Stanley did manage to obtain his pilot's licence. For his contribution to engineering and to the prosperity of Blackburn, Stanley was awarded an M.B.E. and also a doctorate in engineering by Lancaster University. It was probably his lack of formal education which had allowed his mind freedom of movement without restriction.

Dr Stanley Shorrock M.B.E. died in 1989 of a heart attack. He was an entrepreneur of the old school with a zest for life which forced him to pack every minute of it. Without a shadow of doubt he was a pioneer 20 years at least ahead of his time. One of his associates likened him to Colonel "H" Jones of Falklands War fame, a man who could talk to tramps and kings, leaving both with the feeling that they had spoken to someone special.

He was proud of Blackburn, which should be proud of him.

The Russian Connection

George Worledge

What links Blackburn with Moscow's famous Red Square? The answer is architect/painter/sculptor V.O. Sherwood.

Stand in Moscow's Red Square with your back to St. Basil's cathedral, topped by its colourful onion domes, and the Kremlin stretches along on your left. Facing you, occupying the entire other end of the square, is the massive Historical Museum. It is the work of Vladimir Osipovich Sherwood, designed by him some years after his return to Moscow, following his years in Blackburn. The monument to fallen Grenadiers that dominates the centre of Ilinksy Square is also his.

In Russia, Sherwood is inevitably best remembered for such prominent architectural legacies, yet he saw himself first and foremost as a painter. Some of his English paintings, to be seen in the Art Galleries of Blackburn and Preston, certainly confirm his outstanding painterly skill, as also do portraits still in the private possession of Sherwood descendants in Moscow today.

How is it that so famous a Russian should have such an English name? It is because his grandfather, Basil Sherwood was, indeed, English. He came to St. Petersburg at the end of the 18th century, as *"Court Mechanic"*, on the invitation of Czar Paul 1st to bring a breath of Industrial Revolution into Russia.

Vladimir's parents both died young. So he was brought up in a rather special orphanage, of which his aunt was a governor. Here his artistic talent was soon recognised and given every encouragement. Later he graduated from the academy at St. Petersburg, returned to the family house in Moscow, and pursued a busy career.

What made Vladimir come to Blackburn? The invitation of his good friend Charles Dickenson, son of Willian Dickenson, the inventor of the Blackburn loom. Charles had spent some time at the Dickenson's trading office in Moscow.

At the time, Vladimir, aged 27, was recovering from a nervous breakdown due to over-work. Charles persuaded him the sea voyage and the change would do him good. He came. He brought his wife and little daughter and stayed for five years, living in rented accommodation at 7 Princess Road, now demolished. Between their arrival in 1860 and their departure in 1865, the Sherwoods made close friends, not only with the Dickensons, but also with the brothers George and Thomas Ainsworth, who ran Blackburn's Grammar School.

The Blackburn that Sherwood knew was very different from the city today. His diary, as befits an artist, paints vivid pictures in words. Often he is moved by scenes and customs, taken for granted by the English of the day, but fascinatingly strange to him with his Russian background. For example, he admires the way that streets are smoothly surfaced, thanks to Macadam, while, out of town, roads are often hedged by flowering shrubs, and many cottages have roses round their doors and ivy-clad walls.

He is rather amused by the seeming reverence with which the Sunday joint of roast beef is ceremonially carved by the father of the family at table. It prompts him to think that, for the English, roast beef somehow symbolises the nation's greatness. Hence the fervour with which they sing their 'hymn' *"The Roastbeef of Old England."*

Sherwood was saddened by the addiction to alcohol of so many respectable ladies. *"It is the price they pay"*, he writes, *"for a convention of polite society."* He is referring to the custom of making a daily round of social calls. At each call the lady was given a glass of port and a biscuit, which she could not politely refuse. Five or six calls a day could so easily make a lady come to rely on drink.

Then there was the strangeness of English houses. He was astonished at their orderly cleanliness. Not only in their living quarters, he points out, but even in the kitchens. What with their separate larders, and special cellars for wine and coal, *"... it makes life so easy, that sometimes it is even possible to do without servants."*

Yes, times have changed. Domestic servants and huge joints of beef on Sundays are no longer part of life as they were in Sherwood's Blackburn. But not all change is for the worse.

Even in those boom years of Lancashire's cotton trade, Sherwood reports seeing widespread poverty and hunger. What he could seldom see was any blue sky over Blackburn. Sooty, industrial gloom shrouded most cities. Once, when asked what he thought of Blackburn, he picked up some pipes which were lying on the table, stood them upright, and gesturing towards them, said *"Blackburn"*. Perhaps, by comparison, the present is not so black after all.

38

Edward Hart:
a Blackburn Benefactor

Adrian Lewis

"Edward's work is causing much dissatisfaction to his form-master and I myself am afraid that he is not going to make much of Classics. What are we to be thinking of as a career for the lad?"
This was the content of a letter written about 1892 from Edward Hart's housemaster at Rugby to his father Thomas Hart in Blackburn. The house-master need not have worried. Edward had the family firm to provide him with a job in the future and as for Classics, Edward was to create in Blackburn one of the finest classical collections to be seen.

Thomas Hart was an important employer in Blackburn, the owner of the ropeworks in Lambeth Street. His eldest son, Edward, born in 1878 was sent away to school in Newbury and here too he offered his teachers little sign of his future interest.

His October report for 1888 gives his *"History: Rather poor."* In November it grew worse: *"Seems to attend, with disappointing results."*

In French he had begun the school year at the top of his class but by the end of January his teacher's comment was *"Not much taste for it and does not seem to try very hard."* His Classics teacher at Newbury did not have a high opinion of Edward either. In December, 1890, he wrote, *"He is never brilliant, but gets on slowly and generally works steadily but he has not a clear head and is easily confused."*

Luckily for Edward he did have other interests. A fairly tall boy, he played in the school's main football team. Then in September, 1891, he was sent to Rugby. Here while his teachers continued to criticize his work in classics and modern languages, his mathematics were making quiet progress and in October, 1896, he was admitted to Pembroke College, Cambridge, to study mechanical science.

On graduating, Edward came home to take his place in the family firm. The company had been founded by Edward's great grandfather in 1789 when he built a rope-works near the newly built St John's Church. By Edward's time the rope-works had moved to Lambeth Street on the east side of town but the firm retained for a few years a shop in the town centre, on a site now occupied by Blackburn Library.

With his father's death in 1916, Edward took over the

chairmanship and the position of managing director of the company. He never married. He continued to live at the family house, *Brooklands*, in West Park Road and would travel to work at Lambeth Street on the tram.

His favourite hymn, *Peace, perfect peace*, sums up his simple way of life.

Living in the house with him were his mother (the daughter of J.C. Hutton of Darwen's India Mill), his sister Dora Isabel, and a cook and a housemaid. Edward had a retiring nature and the family, even for those days, were a little old fashioned. They would not have dreamed of going to the theatre. They owned a wireless but rarely used it. It took a great deal of pressure from the cook and the housemaid to persuade the family they ought to invest in a vacuum cleaner.

The passion of Edward's life was his collection. His interest lay in examples of the impressed, the cast, the hand struck, the handwritten and the printed word. He collected books and coins. His pleasure was to retreat to the first floor room he had made his library and spend his time with his manuscripts and coins.

The earliest item in his collection, although he may not have understood its meaning, was a cuneiform clay tablet from Mesopotamia, impressed with the Sumerian language and dating from about 2051 BC or to be more precise, from the 43rd year of the reign of King Shugli. In those days before coinage, taxes could be paid in oxen and officials could be paid and offerings given to the temples through the same means. This tablet lists some oxen which had been issued by the equivalent of the royal treasury.

Edward's collection contains Egyptian hieroglyphic inscriptions on papyrus 3,000 years old. The Greeks and Romans are represented by extensive numbers of coins as well as writing and the Byzantines by handwritten documents and books from the sixth to the eleventh centuries.

The finest of all the books are perhaps the fifty medieval illuminated manuscripts which date from the 13th to the 17th centuries. These include psalters, books of hours and a missal prepared in the year 1400 for a Spaniard who was being made a cardinal.

Although it is the history of lettering that binds the collection together it is the illustrations of the manuscripts and books, from 1250 to the 1900s that catch our attention and the artistry on his thousands of Greek, Roman and British coins struck in bronze, silver and gold.

The historical links of some of Edward's collection are as interesting as their appearance. One of the books used to belong to the Nevilles of Northumerland in the 16th century and in the margins they have written their birthdays and wedding anniversaries. Some of his coins have passed through the hands of famous numismatists: Lord Grantley, Montagu, Seltman and the Rev Thompson-Yates, a former vicar of St. Anne's who died in 1903 from whose collection Edward acquired, amongst other pieces, one of the finest surviving examples of the Petition Crown which the engraver, Thomas Simon (out of work because of the engraving he had previously carried out for Cromwell) submitted to the restored Charles II in a forlorn bid to recover his post at the mint.

One or two incidents suggest that Edward was a little nervous his sister might find out how much he was spending on his hobby. Many of the coin labels, which are round like the coins and fit with them in the storage cabinets, have had triangular slices cut out of them because these would have shown the price of the coin.

On one occasion Edward arrived at Maggs, the well-known book dealers in London, to buy four block-books, (early printed books of the 15th century) and he shocked the staff by opening a brief case containing a vast sum of banknotes, no doubt because he did not want anyone at home to see from the stubs of his cheques how much he had been spending.

Unlike many of his fellow businessmen, Edward never stood for election on the borough council. He deserves to be well remembered. He presented his church, St. Silas', with its large west-window dipicting St. Silas, and St. Peter's, Salesbury, where a relation of his had been the vicar, with a west-window which portrays St. Peter.

One of his finest gifts to the town was intended to be anonymous. When the Feildens of Witton, from their home in rural Oxfordshire, offered the council an option to buy Witton Park. The local council, concerned about its financial balances, demurred, it was Edward who came to the rescue. He offered to pay £35,000 towards the price if the council would pay the rest. £35,000 was a lot of money in 1946.

1946 was the year he died. And that might well have been that. However in his last few years Edward had lent some of his books to Blackburn Museum for display and had even presented a few for the town's collection.

Walter Thomas, the librarian and curator, had struck up a friendship with Edward Hart, so much so that Edward in his will bequeathed his magnificent collection to the people of Blackburn with sufficient money to house it. The collection is housed in Blackburn Museum where, in a gallery named after him, some of the choicest examples from what was the love of Edward's life may be seen on display.

41

Extracts From A Blackburn Notebook

Dorothy Ashburn Canham, a retired teacher, possesses a notebook kept by her great, great grandfather, William Hindle Ashburn. It is an exercise book used by him as an occasional diary. In it he wrote of significant happenings in his life, such as the birth of his eight children between 1832 and 1845 and things concerning the Independent Chapel, Blackburn with which he was connected as a deacon.

Born in 1802, educated at the Charity School in Thunder Alley, he later worked for Henry Sudell as an agent, travelling on business to Manchester.

Following a spell as manager in a cotton mill in Langcliffe during the troubled year of 1826, he became manager for William Eccles at Commercial Mills and then set up in partnership with Thomas Thwaites as Cotton Spinners and Manufacturers at Paradise Mills. He studied Law and joined Neville & Eccles, Attorneys. Becoming a town councillor for Park Ward, he involved himself in the life of the town as a Liberal/Non-Conformist.

The Cotton Famine of 1864 put an end to his prosperity and he died in 1867 unaware of his impending bankruptcy.

1832 December 11th.

This day William Feilden of Feniscowles, Dr. Bowring of London, John Fowden Hindle of Woodfold Park and William Turner of Mill Hill, 4 candidates for the representation of the Borough of Blackburn in the Commons House of Parliament, were put in nomination in the Field behind the Theatre in pursuance of an Act passed during the last Session for a Reform in Commons House of Parliament which conferred upon Blackburn the right of sending 2 members. For the convenience of Polling the Town was divided into 3 Districts called the Eastern, Western & Northern Districts. The number of persons present at the Nomination were supposed to be 15,000 and the show of hands were declared in favour of Bowring & Turner.

1832 December 12th.

Early this morning it was announced that Mr Hindle, one of the

Candidates had declined a contest and the polling proceeded on behalf of the three. At the close of this days Poll the numbers were in favour of Feilden & Bowring. The latter having 11 votes more than Mr. Turner.

1832 December 13th.

The polling was again resumed this morning at 8 o'clock and continued till about 1 o'clock. At 2 o'clock the Returning officer (John Fleming) declared from the Hustings the number of votes for each candidate to be for Mr. Feilden 377, Dr. Bowring 334 & Mr. Turner 347 and was received by the people with great indignation in consequence of the means used by Mr. Turner to secure votes viz. by Bribery & Drink. At this moment the Streets between the Theatre and the bottom of Northgate were filled with a dense mob wrought up to the greatest pitch of excitement. The Special Constables (about 700 in number) armed with Staves and Trunsions were driven by the mob from their posts & had their arms seized and broken and immediately after, the windows of the Bull Inn were demolished and many persons wounded.

"Ah'll Tell Thee Summat"

Harry Hunter

In response to a request to commit his memories to paper, Harry Hunter recalled some of his Blackburn boyhood moments now that he is a retired telephone engineer.

As a young lad in the 20's, I remember all the kids would run errands for their Mams and Aunties, or any neighbours, no bother at all, as sometimes you got a small remuneration, like a jam butty or a piece of cake. Sometimes nothing at all but it didn't matter. People then were friendly and honest, and we were brought up *"reight"*.

My favourite errand was going to the chip shop. There was one round every corner then. It was always nice and warm in there on a winter's day, and the aroma gave you an appetite for the feed to come. Everyone took a basin and they would all be lined up on the chip shop range - all kinds, blue and white stripey ones, brown ones, enamel ones, some cracked, some chipped. There was no problem of whose turn it was - just watch the basins move up until yours was at the front, then you were served. You put your own salt and vinegar on, they were well wrapped up in newspaper, and away home you went. I think chips were 1d and 2d. Fish were ½d, 1d and 2d. There was none of that foreign rubbish sold. We'd never heard of curry or anything like that. I used to like watching the man batter the fish in this big dish of white gluey stuff, and make chips out of potatoes with this big iron thing with a handle on. Then he would pour them into the boiling fat with a great sizzle. I used to feel sorry for the fish. Sometimes he gave us a bag of scraps.

It was the same at the old cook shop. I used to take a big jug for 6d-worth of broth, enough for a family of four. Good stuff too. You could sit down inside and have a large plate of potatoe pie for a penny - with real meat in it too.

"Owd Chipper"

In tales told by countless Blackburn dads to their kids, the name of *"Owd Chipper"* often appears. He was an entertainer on the town's street corners to the town's children. He ran a peep show in the style of *"Punchy & Judy"* to take youngsters into the world of make-believe. How many folk know anything about the man?

Robert Reynolds was born in about 1824 at Cuerden Green, and came to live with his parents in Knuzden when he was a lad of 7 or 8 years. Even then, he was fascinated by the stage, but his parents disapproved of his liking for theatricals. It appears that, whilst a teenager, young Bob heard that a play, *"A Chip Off The Old Block"* had come to the Theatre Royal. Despite the threat of parental violence, our hero went to see it. His father, learning that he had gone into town to see it, thought he would teach him a lesson, and bribed two cronies with a gallon of ale to dress as ghosts. They waited for young Bob on lonely Accrington Road (this would be about 1840) behind a hedge. Their antics didn't frighten him, and his father's mates realised he was, in their words *"a chip off the old block"*, so they called him *"Chipper"* (or perhaps it was because he told them he had seen a play with that title).

Out of work about 1850 through over-drinking, Chipper acquired a large box, mounted it on wheels and fixed two brush handles for shafts. Across, the back of the cart he built what looked like a dog kennel - his peep show. He gave shows in the streets to children in return for a bundle of rags, which he traded in at a *"rag shop"* (today that would be called a *"textile recycling plant"*), and continued to earn his living in this fashion for over fifty years, bringing pleasure to several generations of Blackburn rag-a-muffins. A photograph taken of him was turned into a postcard. Over six thousand copies were sold, many being sent to exiled Blackburners throughout the world.

A more serious Bob Reynolds could recite passages from the writings of Shakespeare. He died on 5th March 1912, aged 88 years.

The Munificent Harrisons

Graham Chadwick

Joseph Harrison arrived in the still little town of Blackburn in 1828 from Ingleton. At 23 he was a skilled engineer who could read and write and he must have had a small sum of capital with which to establish his first smithy in Dandy Walk hard by the parish church - now the cathedral. It was also in the shadow of the state-of-the-art Jubilee Mill with its steam engines and iron-framed looms. Every rough road leading into the town must have been cluttered with heaving carts loaded with stone and the barges on the canal and all the new wharves must have resembled ancient Egypt during the construction of its temples. Mills were going up everywhere and Blackburn was on the point of becoming the greatest weaving centre in the world. Young Joseph could hardly fail. His first profits came from wrought iron gates and railings, and were reinvested in the Bank Foundry at Nova Scotia which manufactured lamp-posts for the new gas comany and later the Corporation. But it was the casting and construction of looms which was overwhelmingly the most important part of his business. This was hi-tech industry and Lancashire has to be seen as the latter day California. Pennine valleys were *"silicon valleys"*. Why else would the most talented and enterprising young men from everywhere in England and beyond have settled here?

Iron Street, at one time known as Harrison Street, off Bolton Road, is the only reminder we have left of the Bank Foundry but the recently scrubbed and polished Soho Foundry building at Salford was set up by one of Harrison's moulders, John Dugdale, one of a new generation of ironmasters who left Joseph to make their own fortunes. This was a time of stupendous growth when orders had to be turned away and capital was cheap. One of Joseph's looms was exhibited at Crystal Palace in 1851. Some would say this event marked the beginning of the end for Lancashire as now the world was *"cottoning on"*. For example, during March 1852 over 40 rail wagons heavily loaded with looms, sizing and warping machines and other apparatus, enough to equip an extensive factory, were dispatched to Sweden from the Bank Foundry. And the staggering fact is that this represented a mere eight days production. With this wealth he acquired the Highfield Mill, Nova Scotia Mill and

Witton Mill. The blacksmith had become a cotton baron of the first rank, still living, incredibly until 1847, in a cramped terraced house next door to the Bank Foundry where today stands the Moorings Public house.

But a cotton baron was a public figure of political as well as economic importance and needed a more fitting residence. Joseph and his family moved into Gallingreaves Hall. This was not an imposing country seat such as those into which many of his contemporaries chose in order to assert their status as members of the new ruling class. It is best described as *"a large suburban villa"*. Certainly it was grander then, set in its own wooded grounds, than today when it is a scruffy public house, hemmed in by the terraced houses built for the labourers in all the other mills built in that area between 1850 and 1900.

Joseph was either very modest or afraid to go and live more than walking distance from his factories. He did buy his baronial mansion eventually; Salmesbury Old Hall in 1862 which he restored to its original Fifteenth century splendour. He never went to live there, giving it instead to his eldest son, William.

The Harrisons represented new money and the new bourgeoisie. They and others like them who had *"made themselves"* challenged and outwitted the old money represented by families like the Feildens, lords of the manor and members of parliament for generations past. It seemed to the new men a nonsense that a great town like Blackburn should have no unitary and democratic system of local government. In 1852 the granting of the Charter of Incorporation of the Borough and the holding of the first municipal elections sealed their triumph. Almost inevitably, Joseph was elected. He became a J.P. and deputy lieutenant of the county. He was offered the mayoralty every year for the rest of his life but always refused. Instead he donated a gold mayoral chain to the Borough, (the one that was stolen in 1982). Was he overly modest? Was he always at heart a simple blacksmith? We have a reminiscence of Luke Walsmsley describing Joseph towards the end of his life -

"Old Joe - I see him at this moment, passing by in the street, singularly indifferent as to his clothes, so honestly begrimed of the foundry. I have often seen him pick up odd bits of iron from the road for the scraphead of his furnace."

He died in 1880 aged 75, a great man though he must have been a hard man to work for.

Of his three son, the youngest, Henry, was the one who carried on old Joe's work. Although perhaps insufficient acknowledgement has been made to the middle son, John, who took on much of the humdrum day-to-day administration of the firm. Henry spread himself and was much less reluctant than his father to stand in the public spotlight. It was Henry who, at the age of 17, represented the Harrisons at the Great International Exhibition in the Crystal Palace in 1851 and for the rest of his life he spent as much time away from the business as he did in running it. He became the salesman and ambassador, not only of the Harrisons but of Blackburn commerce and Lancashire industry. For a quarter of a century he travelled to every country in Europe, to India, China, Russia, America and Egypt multiplying and strengthening the threads which bound the Empire in a web of cotton. We do not know what wild oats he sowed whilst he carried the flag around the world but he did not marry until 1872 when he was 38 and his wife, Maude, not much younger. This is probably why they were childless and both devoted their energies towards *"good works"* thereafter.

Henry was elected to the town council in 1877 and immediately elevated to the aldermanic bench. By 1880 - he was mayor wearing the chain given by Old Joe. It would have been interesting to see both Joseph and Henry sitting on the magistrates bench handing down fines and prison sentences to cotton rioters, some of whom must have been their own employees.

In 1877 together with Edgar Appleby and Eli Heyworth, Henry founded the Blackburn Chamber of Commerce, of which he remained president until his death. He presented the Chamber with its suite of offices in Richmond Terrace and established its dynamic, outward-looking tradition by sending out trade missions all round the world, most notably the one to China in 1896 which took over a year and penetrated deep into territories almost unknown to outsiders.

It was customary then for cotton manufacturers to make frequent rail trips to warehouses and to the Exchange in Manchester and Henry set up the first telephone link between his Blackburn factories and Manchester to obviate many of these tiresome journeys.

A by-product of the Chinese expedition was a campaign by Henry and the brewing magnate Yerburgh to foster the teaching of Chinese. They were instrumental in the foundation of a Chair in Chinese at London University in 1901 and courses at Manchester University supported by £1,000 for scholarships.

By the turn of the century almost every aspect of Blackburn life was benefiting from Harrison *"munificence"*. (That is the word inscribed on the memorial tablet to Maude Harrison in the Harrison Institute).

The Infirmary received furniture, the latest X Ray equipment and regular gifts for all its staff and patients. The Workshops for the Blind, Mrs. Lewis' Teetotal Mission, the new Technical School and the old School of Art were a few of the dozens of beneficiaries. Perhaps because they had no direct heirs the Harrisons were so generous then. The giving became so regular and diverse that they set up a body specifically to regulate it — *"the Charity Organisation Society"*, at *"Harrison House"*, 12 Simmons Street. Between 1900 and 1914 over £100,000 was channelled through this office.

The Borough recognised and rewarded such munificence by granting Henry the Freedom of Blackburn in 1909.

His last gifts were those made in his will in 1914. His estate amounted to £344,861.14s.0d. From this he left £82,300 to local and national charities in the form of 35 separate legacies of between £1,000 and £5,000. Naval and marine charities took quite a big chunk as did cancer research bodies. He left £2,000 for playing fields for the grammar school, £1,600 to the workshops for the blind and £1,000 for the Female Mission for the Fallen.

Today most Blackburnians know best the Harrison Gymnasium and the Harrison Girls' Institute. When Joseph died the grounds of Galligreaves Hall, which were quite extensive, had already been reduced by the erection of several terraces of workmens' dwellings. Henry and Maude had settled in a house at the top of Preston New Road, 'Stanley', and the Galligreave grounds were now sold off for the building of Stansfeld, Hancock, Wellington and the other streets in the vicinity. However three open spaces were reserved for public use. One became the Hollin Bridge Street Recreation Ground and the others were the sites for the Gymnasium and the Institute with gardens and tennis courts. The Institute provided both a vocational and liberal education for young women right from its opening in 1910 and it must have fulfilled a major role in the emancipation of the women of Blackburn throughout this century.

The Harrisons were fortunate in being in the right place at the right moment of history but they were real people who you might see in the street, not absentee capitalists removing themselves and their money to balmy tax havens. Their memorials are colleges, hospitals, playing fields. As their family motto has it, they gave, *"Not rashly nor with fear."*

Blackburn In The Cotton Famine

The effects of Lancashire in the North-v-South war in America have been well documented. In brief, it was that no raw cotton came here, the mills were silent and the workers starved. No town felt these effects more than Blackburn, whose whole well-being depended upon American cotton alone.

The war soon brought pressure upon the town, and on 10th April 1862, the Mayor, Robert Hopwood Hutchinson, wrote on behalf of the Relief Committee which had been formed:-

An Appeal on behalf of the distressed operatives of Blackburn

It may not be generally known that severe distress and privations are being suffered by the operatives and others employed in the manufacturing districts of Lancashire.

No place or district suffers more from this distress than Blackburn where the population are extensively employed in the cotton trade which has for a long time been in a depressed condition.

For many months past, most if not all the mills have been working little more than half time, and now when the savings of the operatives have been exhausted a larger number of the mills are closed, and the labouring manufacturing population are unable to obtain even partial employment, and with exhausted resources are dependant upon the Poor Rates and the gifts of the charitable for their existence.

It is evident that as thousands of the population of Blackburn have now become entirely destitute, neither the Poor Law Guardians nor any other Body can adequately grapple with the difficulty alone and unaided.

To assist in relieving the distress, a subscription list has been opened, and a fund realised of nearly £2,500 from donations of £100 each down to small sums.

A soup kitchen was established in January last and since then a daily distribution has been made of from 1500 to 2000 quarts.

Bread and oat meal are also distributed weekly amongst needy objects, and the committee are already expending about £200 per week in relieving from nine to ten thousand people, and as the distress not only continues but is on the increase, it is estimated it will now require a weekly expenditure of a still larger amount to make the income of each recipient equal to one shilling per head per week.

The funds are rapidly decreasing, and the local claims are almost exhausted, hence the committee feel it is imperatively necessary to appeal to the charitable for further aid in order that they may continue to relieve the prevailing distress.

The serious losses incurred in running their mills prevent millowners from contributing as largely and generously to the fund as they otherwise would, and this circumstance deprives the committee of a considerable source of supply, and in like manner effects the ability to contribute of the various Gentry, Tradespeople and operatives connected with and interested in this town.

Any benevolent person who will kindly assist the committee will have their donations gratefully acknowledged and the funds carefully distributed to needy and deserving persons.

John Fielden, Honorary Secretary to the Relief Committee issued a report on the state of the town at the end of May 1862. It made depressing reading:-

There are 25 mills entirely stopped ... 7,127 (hands) are working full time, 8,215 short time and 7,238 out of work ... It is now 42 weeks since short time working really commenced in the large establishments ... it appears there is a total loss to the operatives of £10,081.2s weekly ... Throughout the crisis the operatives have been orderly and peaceful. Crime is on the decrease while poverty has been terribly on the increase. It is a common thing to have a maiden sessions before our magistrates, and the borough petty cases are decreased by hundreds as compared with the same period in previous years.

BLACKBURN TECHNICAL SCHOOL.

✤ PROPOSED ✤
TECHNICAL & TRADE SCHOOL
FOR BLACKBURN AND DISTRICT.

IT is probably well known throughout Blackburn and District that the GENERAL PURPOSES COMMITTEE of the Corporation of Blackburn have decid.d in favour of the establishment .of a TECHNICAL and TRADE SCHOOL FOR BLACKBURN and DISTRICT as the best means of locally celebrating the JUBILEE of the reign of ¹Ier Majesty the QUEEN, and have ⁀requested the MAYOR OF BLACKBURN to convene a TOWN'S MEETING on the subject. This meeting will be held on WEDNESDAY, the 9th instant, at 7-30 p.m., in the TOWN HALL, Blackburn.

In view of this meeting, the undersigned have been requested to prepare and circulate this handbill, with the view of setting forth concisely some of the advantages to be derived from the establishment of the proposed School.

The main object of the School will be to enable artisans in every branch of trade and manufacture, and their Children, and others of limited means, to acquire a thorough practical knowledge of the principles of their respective trades or manufactures, special regard, of course, being had to the Textile and other Staple Industries of this District.

It is a matter of common knowledge that Foreign Countries throughout the world are daily entering into greater competition with British Manufactures in our own Markets and in Markets which are not protected by hostile tariffs, and it is the opinion of many of the ablest men of the day that this competition, if not wholly induced, is at any rate greatly increased, by the education given in the TECHNICAL SCHOOLS which many of our foreign competitors have largely established in their midst.

At present, for example, in this District a young workman with every wish and desire to improve his knowledge has no adequate opportunity within his means of doing so; if these Schools are established he will be able to obtain thorough instruction in Weaving and Pattern Designing, Carpentry and Joinery, Building Construction, Steam, Applied Mechanics, Practical Chemistry, Electricity, Telegraphy, and in every branch of Trade or Science that may be called for: and the result of increased knowledge must be to the benefit, not only of the Student, but of the Trade in which he is concerned, and to all connected with it.

In order to establish Schools at all worthy of the occasion, a sum of at least £25,000 will be required to be raised. The MAYOR OF BLACKBURN has generously offered to head the Subscription List with a donation of £500, and other gentlemen in the district have also generously offered similar and other Subscriptions; but, if the scheme is to be a success, and the money is to be raised, everyone must take an interest in it, and be prepared to make some sacrifices to aid it.

We earnestly invite your attendance at the Town's Meeting above mentioned, and hope to have your cordial co-operation. The Meeting will be addressed by Mr. MATHER, of Salford, and other Gentlemen.

HENRY HARRISON.
ELI HEYWORTH,
W. E. L. GAINE.
J. B. Mc.CALLUM.

Blackburn, Feb. 1st, 1887.

TIMES OFFICE, BLACKBURN.

What's Been Said About Blackburn

Collected by Stanley Miller & Bob Dobson

Blackbourne, a market town on the East side of Lancashire, is surrounded by parks and forests, such as Hoghton, Samlesbury, Osbaldestone, Salesbury and Walton-in-le-Dale, all in the Hundred of that place. The Darwen runs a little to the South of Blackburn, and then winds away to the West and mixes with the Ribble at Walton-in-le-Dale.

R. Lambarde (Topographer) 1570

I rode ten miles from Bury to Blackburn, and from the hills had a fine view of the country to the South East. It is a town which thrives by the cotton and woollen manufacture. On these hills I saw some Coal Pits and a Quarry of good freestone near Blackburne. At this town there is a fair Free School in the Churchyard; and Mr. Hoadley has a grand house here, who I think, made his fortune by the cotton and linen manufacture carried on there. I ascended the hills, and on the top of them had a glorious view towards Wigan, Preston and the sea on the one hand, and towards Clitheroe, Gisburn, Pendle Hill and Yorkshire on the other. I descended to the Ribchester Bridge over the Ribble, and soon came to Ribchester.

Richard Pococke (Traveller and Explorer) 1750

Sir Robert Peel's father was a small farmer in the neighbourhood of Blackburn, and was in the habit of bringing milk into Blackburn daily. The manufacturers spun and wove their own goods, carrying them on their backs on foot into Yorkshire and other places for sale. There was no conveyance between Blackburn and Manchester but one cart. I used to drink and eat all sorts of stuff, but did not sit up all night until one or two o'clock in the morning as many persons do. It was not common to marry before they were 34 or 35 years of age.

Joseph Bolton (Handloom Weaver and Centenarian) 1760

Blackburn, the capital of a district that formerly had the addition of "Shire". The whole territory was bestowed by William the Conqueror on Ilbert De Lacy. The town is situated in a valley or bottom surrounded by hills; it is at present rising into greatness, resulting from the overflow of Manufacturers from Manchester.

The manufactures are cottons - considerable quantities are printed here; others are sent to London. The fields around are whitened with the materials which are bleached on them. The streets are irregular; but some good houses, that effect of wealth, begin to appear here and there in several places.

Thomas Pennant (Antiquarian and Naturalist) 1776

The form of this parish is irregular; its greatest length fron North East to South West is about fourteen miles, and its breadth exceeds ten miles. ... The township of Blackburn in 1802 contained 11,980 persons, which is more than double the number it contained in 1782, occasioned by the prosperous trade of the place. ... Three fairs are held in this town, viz. at Easter, May Day and Michaelmas; it also has a market every Wednesday and Saturday, and a police for regulating the market and for paving, watching and cleansing the streets. ... Little can be said on behalf of the state of agriculture in this parish. Estates are generally divided into small farms, for the purpose of supplying the farmer, who is generally a weaver, with milk and butter for his family. It is by the loom chiefly that rents are paid. ... The grain most commonly grown is oats. Neither the climate, nor the soil are favourable to the cultivation of wheat.

Thomas Starkie (Vicar of Blackburn) 1807

Blackburn contains 15,083 inhabitants, chiefly employed in the manufacturing business. There are three churches, viz. Old Church, St. John's lately built, and St. Paul's, and several meeting houses for dissenters. ... It is remarkable that there is not a single sheep farm in the parish, the market being supplied with beef and mutton from the rich pastures of Craven. The modern mansion of Henry Feilden, Esq., is less than two miles from Blackburn. It is built of cream-coloured freestone, and has in front a portico supported by Doric pillars. At Woodfold near Blackburn, also, a very magnificent house has been erected by Henry Sudell, Esq., of bluish-grey stone.

George A. Cooke (Geographer) 1814

I am sorry to say that the distress in this place has abated not at all, but is on the increase. There is no advance in wages for handloom weavers. The present wages for weavers will not be more than 3s. or 3s. 6d. a week.

Robert Dobson (Minister, Great Harwood) 1820

Blackburn is a Market Town and Parish in the Hundred of Blackburn, 23 miles NNW of Manchester and 209 miles NW by N of London. Of the 9,795 families in this parish, 552 are chief engaged in agriculture; and 8,506 in trade, manufactures or handicraft.

The parish church of Blackburn, dedicated to St. Mary, was founded and endowed before the Norman conquest. ... About five years ago it was found necessary to take down the whole structure, and the church is now rebuilding upon the site of the ancient Grammar School. The steeple is still standing, together with the chapel of the Duncan family, which contains the altar, and in which the ceremonies of baptism and marriage are performed, as well as the funeral service. In addition to the parish church there are two modern churches of the establishment, St. John's and St. Peter's, and a chapel St. Paul's in which the services according to the rites of the Church of England are performed by a preacher in Lady Huntington's community. The dissenting chapels are ten in number ... there is a second Roman Catholic Chapel building in Brook House Field. ...

The number of cotton pieces manufactured in Blackburn weekly is now estimated at 49,200, the workmanship of which gives employment to 10,000 persons, and the annual value of these goods before they are dyed and printed is calculated at two millions sterling ... and there are now about 100,000 spindles at work in the town and its immediate vicinity, which yield an average weight of yarn of about 35,000 lb. weekly.

Edward Baines (Historian) 1824

The power-loom being introduced and hundreds of old handloom weavers as a consequence are thrown out of employment. About two-thirds of the work force in the Blackburn district are in a state of absolute indigence. About the beginning of the present year, 1828, the Rev. Dr. Stewart of Liverpool, the Rev. George Brown of Holcombe, and the Rev. William McKerrow of Manchester having heard that the Chapel in Mount Street was unoccupied, probably to be found in the inability of the people to support the ordinances, waited upon the proprietor, Mrs. Grime, and entered into arrangements for opening it and retaining it as a place of worship in connection with the United Association Synod. The worshippers were pleased with the ministrations of the preachers, and desired to be formed into a congregation of the Secession Church ... Dr. Stewart wrote to London Presbytery to appoint one of their number to organise the congregation, and place in under the Presbytery. His request was granted, and he was appointed by the Presbytery to this work. In conformity with the appointment, Rev. Dr. Stewart officiated at Mount Street Chapel on the 7th September, 1828. Extracted from the Minutes of Presbytery.

William Broadfoot (Presbyterian Historian) 1828

Shear Brow was an important highway, and the old *Hole i'th'*
Wall was a well-known house of call. My father kept a team of pack
donkeys at Lane Ends. These donkeys were used for carrying sand
in their panniers from Sunnyhurst to Darwen and Tockholes, and
taking back coal. At the end of a day's journey, he stopped at the
Hole i'th' Wall for a camp, leaving the donkeys on the highway. I
used to bring them home. Seats were placed in front of the hotel where
men sat smoking their churchwardens and drinking *Old Ben.*

Mrs Annie Hayhurst (Weaver) 1830

Blackburn was long famous for its goods, cotton goods, formerly
known by the name of *Blackburn checks*, which consisted of a linen
warp shot with a cotton woof, one or both of which being dyed in the
thread, gave to the piece when woven a striped or checked
appearance. This article was superceded by the *Blackburn greys*, so
called from their colour, neither the warp nor the woof being dyed
before they put into the loom ... These goods are generally sent to
London to be printed. A greater change took place when the greys
were substituted by calicoes, in which the whole fabric is cotton,
and which owe their name to their resemblance to the cotton cloth
of India, brought from the province of Calicat. The printing of
calicoes now forms a considerable part of the business of
Blackburn...

The New Lancashire Gazetteer 1830
(similar to Britton The Beauties of England & Wales 1807)

There is a greater proportion of the uneducated classes in
Blackburn than in Preston, and the passion for liquor is a source of
ruin and disgrace ....

Rev. J. Clay, chaplain of Preston Gaol, 1833

With all its natural advantages of soil and position, and not
withstanding its happy exemption from many of the evils by which
other places are afflicted, the town of Blackburn possesses one
monster nuisance, which more than neutralises all the benefits to
which I have alluded. Your readers will perceive by anticipation
that I now refer to that black, murky, slimy, filthy sink of
abomination, egregiously misnamed a brook that, like a poisonous
serpent seems to envelope the town in its sinuous and deadly folds.
Well is the town called Blackburn if the etymology of its name is to
be traced to that foul and fetid agglomeration of nastiness - that
lethiferous, stygian burn on whose gloomy margin so many of our
inhabitants have the misfortune to be domiciled.

Issac Lloyd in a letter to "The Blackburn Standard" 5.8.1846

For six months of the year, Blackburn stands upon the river Blakewater; for the other six months when there is no water, black or other, in the channel of that stream, it stands upon its merits, or on nothing, which, however is much the same thing .... It possesses a Mayor, and the majority of the inhabitants have corporations. It is a rambling, scattered and dishevelled looking place; something like the Devil-fish in Victor Hugo's novel. It has a compact black centre, and pushes out longer or shorter limbs in every direction. During the last thirty years its increase has been enormous and as it has increased precisely as anybody chose, mills and cottages being run up anywhere and anyhow, it will be one of the very worse places in Lancashire to improve into shape. One third of the entire constituency are keepers of beerhouses, and the aristocracy of the place are brewers. It is therefore needless to say that it is a thorough-going Tory community. Strong drink is the secret of its own and Britain's greatness; after that its heart has been given for long years to the church and cockfighting. Be sober, lead a reputable life, keep a decent and moderate tongue in your head, and our genuine Blackburner will wax red at the mention of your name and dismiss you as *"a --Dissenter"* ... One of the most noticeable facts in Blackburn is the almost total absence of gentlemen among its people ... No Manchester merchant dreams of doubting the word of a Blackburn man.

"The Free Lance" October 1867

No town owes more to the energy of its people and the public spirit of its local government, and none could give more striking proof of the talents and capabilities of the men of Lancashire.

Unknown journalist, 1896

* * *

J.B. Priestley called Blackburn *"a sad-looking town"* in his book *"English Journey"* (1934). In 1935, Miss K. Dummerfield took him to task for his pessimistic views on the town in the Blakev Moor Girls School magazine.

* * *

The streets of Lancashire that I remember were parades of gleaming window sills and doorsteps pummelled with weekly applications of donkey-stone. Unlike Mr Priestley I did not - do not - find such townscape ugly. There was a touching beauty about the long rows of two-storey cots laced in a compact urban web - the rhythm of purple rooflines weaving down the sides of the dark bowl that was Blackburn - a bravado in the clusters of mill chimneys at the bottom, each stack an ingenious variation of the bricklayer's art.

I used to set out on my boyhood explorations after breakfast when the trams had started down at '*t'Boolyvard*' outside the soot-black railway station. Blunt-nosed barges would be gliding on the green canal, moss flourishing between the backlane setts, a few ragmen already keening.

It was then I used to hear the buckets, grey iron pails galvanised with zinc, handles rattling. There was the slosh of water hurled across the rust-brown pavements, the swish of stiff yardbrooms - ten or twenty thousand housewives '*dooin' thur fronts*', scrubbing the very streets outside their homes, swilling down the sides of the bowl of Blackburn, the morning ritual.

'*Goodmornin' Miss Rimmin'ton ... Goodmornin' Missis Smith ... Goodmornin' ...*'

The right approach to Blackburn is across the moors touching the old shire of sheep and hursts that was woollen country before it took in Irish flax then US cotton. So when I'd taken breakfast and paid for my night's berth I took the high road.

As I approached a sprawling suburb I stopped to ask three girls if I was still on course. Two stood back a pace, grinning from their pert industrial faces. Their spokesman, a pretty lass, answered boldly in the dialect that still has traces of Celt, the Angle and the Norseman immigrant. Her face, though, was from far away - like as not Kwangtung - and her eyes were almond-shaped.

The road slid down between houses of brick and rough, rain-darkened stone from either side ran once-familiar streets. I parked in one of them and made my way on foot. About me were all the roof-shapes, ventilators, warehouse entrances that had first enchanted me as a boy of nine or ten. I recognised small details instantly and knew that here I had formed tastes and attitudes that still existed. But I could no longer make an intimate connection. The boy and I were strangers. Too much had happened in between.

I looked for Bicknell Street where I had spent one August with an unmarried aunt who stuffed me with Rowntree's chocolate and plied me with cinema money she could ill afford. But something quite remarkable had taken place. The woman on a doorstep looking right and left had not the pinched face of a millgirl-housewife, a dedicated pavement scrubber. She was more self-contained, more placid. Her cheeks and jaw-line were less angular. She was taller and had a darker skin. The solemn little girls who

59

graced the streets were not the skinny imps - the Lizzies and Mary-Ellens - I had known. The small shopping streets were animated now, crowded, more colourful and prosperous than I recalled. Where there had been black woollen shawls there were saris. There were exotic names above store windows and different, spicier smells came from the doorways.

As in a dream, my quest became compulsive. I *had* to find the place. I saw two Englishwomen chatting on a corner. *"Which way for Bicknell Street?"* They looked at one another before they gathered wit to answer a tall young man addressed me. *"Excuse me,"* he said. His speech was faintly Lancashire, his manner courteous. He looked like a technical college student. *"Excuse me - did you say you wanted Bicknell Street? I am walking that way. Would you care to come along?"* As he strode on he said, *"I know Bicknell Street quite well. I'm just going their for a bit pray."*

Bicknell Street was as steep as I remembered. It climbed to a brow beyond which, out of sight, the residences of clerks and middle-class insurance men, then the mill bosses, were said to be. The chapel a few doors up from where my aunt had lived, and into which my guide now disappeared with a grave goodbye, had been turned into a mosque.

Frank Entwisle "Abroad in England" (Andre Deutsch 1982)

Blackburn and the Women's Movement

Stanley Miller

Although the Blackburn branch of the Women's Movement was formed in 1895 while the Pankhursts were still working in Manchester, becoming a branch of the *Women's Political and Social Union* in 1903, Blackburn was not regarded as very active in Women's Suffrage matters.

Upper class women were more interested in social and welfare work, such as visiting cases on behalf of the *Charity Organisation Society* (formed February 7th, 1895) and arranging socials to provide funds for the *District Nursing Association* (founded April 28th, 1896). Another activity in which they were involved was the supply of free meals to necessitous children in 1904.

While upper-class Blackburn was male dominated, and content to be so, in certain working-class areas, women were the dominant sex. A canvasser on behalf of Philip Snowden in the 1900 Election was surprised to find a Grimshaw Park husband polishing the brass knocker on his front door, and sandstoning the door step and window sills. Another elector in the same area consulted his wife before announcing that he would take her advice and continue to vote Tory. The explanation probably lies in the fact that women could find more certain and secure work as four-loom weavers than their husbands, since in many mills boys were turned off on reaching 18 or 21 and forced to take outdoor work liable to seasonal unemployment. Since the wife earned more, she took over the usual male role.

There were reckoned to be 120 working mothers in Blackburn and agitations were started in the early 1900's for day nurseries or creches. Day nurseries had been organised earlier in St. Peter's district by Rev. G.E. Hignett, and by Eli Heyworth at Audley in the 1890's. The latter had been unsuccessful as it was reserved for employees of Audley Hall Mills, and when work people moved out of the district it was no longer convenient for them, so the number of the children attending declined and the nursery closed. It was felt that a nursery organised on district lines, and not confined to workers from a single mill would have been successful.

The numbers of Blackburn women workers was at a peak in 1911, when 18,372 Blackburn resident women textile workers were in employment.

Theresa Billington commented on the lack of interest in Women's Suffrage in Blackburn shortly after her marriage in January 1907. - *"20 Lancashire women have gone to jail. Is not Blackburn going to send some representative to show the earnestness of the women in the Town!"* Miss Adela Pankhurst and Mrs. Snowden addressed a meeting on Women's Suffrage at the Lees Hall, on February 4th, 1907. Louisa Entwistle presided on this occasion, and she was shortly to give Blackburn's answer to Theresa Billington's taunt. Hitherto, Louisa, of 133 Burnley Road, had continued her work at the mill, and addressed meetings at or near the mills. However on February 11th, 1907 she was called up on active duty by Emmeline Pankhurst, arriving in London late the same day. On February 12 she was one of the delegates lobbying the House of Commons, and on being arrested by the Police, charged and convicted, refused to pay the fine, and elected to go to jail instead.

During the same year, 1907, the force of the movement in Blackburn was dissipated by the formation of breakaway and rival movements - the *Women's Labour League* on February 19; the *Women's Liberal League*; and the *Women's Suffrance Society* on December 8th. This splintering was reflected nationally by Theresa Billington's *Women's Freedom League* of September, 1907.

The cause was also discredited to some extent by a forged letter signed *'Louise Entwistle'* claiming the support for the women of Sir Harry Hornby, the local Conservative, which was promptly denied by Sir Harry's Agent. Louisa's father proved that the letter was not from his daughter, and the signature *'Louise'* instead of *'Louisa'*, but the harm was done.

There was also considerable anti-suffrage feeling which was voiced by D.J. Shackleton, M.P.:- *"The Factory Act provided that women should not go to work before one month after the birth of a child. Married women should stay at home. Mill life for women means ready made dinners, and tasty scraps instead of wholesome food."* Opposition found a more active form in the *Anti-Women's Suffrance League*, founded in Blackburn on April 5th, 1907.

During the early part of 1907 came a trade depression, with 157 applications for relief to the *Blackburn Distress Committee, while later in the year there was agitation for a 5% pay increase for textile workers. Both these events sapped the strength of the movement.*

1908 saw a meeting of the *Women's Liberal League,* and on November 25th there was a demonstration for Women's Suffrage at the Town Hall. This annual event each November was becoming the main method of keeping the cause alive. The meeting on November 27, 1911 was addressed by Lady Frances Balfour. Now another weakening effect came from an agitation by trade unions for their members not to work alongside non-unionists in the Cotton Mills. This resulted in a General Lockout, but not in 100% union membership.

Local women were so incensed at the way Blackburn Corporation was managing its affairs - their policy had led to a strike of gas-workers from January 1st 1914, that they held a protest meeting on January 28th. This same year saw the only event of the *"direct action"* campaign by the Women's Suffrance movement. On March 15th, the cannon in Corporation Park was found to have its touch-hole and part of the barrel filled with gun-powder, a long fuse being attached. Luckily none exploded. A quantity of Suffragette literature was spread around.

Militant and other activities ceased on the outbreak of War. Blackburn women found fresh outlets attending Belgian wounded, and later British, at Ellerslie Hospital. They worked on the railway, as tram drivers and conductors, and in heavy industry. They were duly rewarded by the vote at the end of World War I in 1918.

Blackburn Weavers in the Latter Half of the 19th Century

Justine Cotton

(Conclusions reached in an essay submitted for a degree to the University of Exeter, 1991)

Blackburn's prominence as a producer of cotton cloth and centre for ideas with the cotton industry made it an important and indispensable part of the industry. While cotton was the pacemaker for industrial change, so Blackburn was the place where many of its parts were assembled. Blackburn was successful in contributing to improvements in both spinning and weaving machinery. (For example, the Spinning Jenny in 1764, and the Blackburn Plain Loom in 1827). But just as the cotton industry's role in the industrialization of Britain is often overestimated, so too can Blackburn's role within the industry. Bolton, Bury, Preston, Doncaster and Stockport, and others besides, also shared in the early improvements to cotton machinery. Blackburn did, however, become the world's main centre of cloth production, and housed the largest group of weavers in the country. For this reason Blackburn can undoubtedly be known as the most important cotton weaving town in Lancashire.

Blackburn was not only important within Lancashire, but for the U.K. economy. Its contribution to U.K. cotton exports in 1850 were as much as 40%. However, while the period was one of general growth, it was also one of relative decline; its contribution in 1896 had fallen to 29%. Blackburn served as an indicator of the cotton industry's national performance. The U.K. share in world cotton goods exported also dropped from a peak of 82% in 1882-4 to 58% in 1910-13.

The cause of this decline appeared to be the increasing competition from Europe and America, as they caught up with England's technology. Blackburn, however, was quick to take the lead in exploiting the new colonial markets, and became the main centre for the vast Indian and Chinese Trade.

Blackburn's economic contibutions both regionally and nationally were, therefore, substantial but its importance on the social development of the weavers cannot be denied. The Blackburn

Weavers' Association (1854) - probably formed in retaliation to the establishment of the Employers' Association in 1852 - played an important role in terms of maintaining the Blackburn Standard Wage Rate, and campaigning for improvements in working conditions. The fruits of its activities were throughout Lancashire. By 1883, the Blackburn List regulated nearly two thirds of wages earned upon 600,000 powerlooms, and in 1892 it became the basis of the new list which replaced all other local lists.

Blackburn took the leading role in the industrial relations of the Lancashire cotton operatives. They acted as either supporters to operatives in other towns, or as the leaders in widespread industrial disputes. It appears that many towns felt it was satisfactory to accept the result achieved by the Blackburn Association, rather than face a disruption of trade in their own town. Indeed by 1900, it was estimated that Blackburn Weavers' Association had at least 10,700 members although in 1889 the Association itself put the figure over 11,000. The national figure for organized workers stood at something like half a million. If such a crude comparison can be made, Blackburn's share in the number of organized workers was as much as 2%.

It is generally accepted that the working class saw a relative improvement in many of its conditions over the period. Blackburn undoubtedly saw improvements in real wages. In 1900, they were 33% above their 1875 level, and 84% higher than in 1850. However, this study does help to show that for many, life remained harsh. Living standards were far from satisfactory.

The shape of the weavers' lives was changed by mechanization and the rise of the factory in the late nineteenth century. They had problems and activities, failures and achievements, but it is their changes in attitudes which seems to have characterized the period more than any other. The weavers' (eventually) consented support towards the building of the Technical College in the 1890's is perhaps a benchmark between the attitudes of old, and the beginnings of more modern thinking.

Whereas before they had destroyed new technology, now they consented to educate men to design it, in the hope that it would lead to larger orders and improve the manufacturers' position. This is surely an indication of a remarkable transformation in the mentality and in the lives of the English working class within the cotton textile industry.

Grimshaw Park Reflections

James A. Marsden

The origins of Grimshaw Park stem from the founding of a sandstone quarry, by royal assent in 1618. St. Mary's and St. Joseph's R.C. Junior school, Bennington St. - in part - now occupies this site. The dwellings which adjoined the excavation, were roughly formed into two lines towards the highway bound for Bury, they became known as *Jack Croft*.

The homesteads were built of the stone for and by the men who worked the quarry. It was said that many of these had travelled from Haslingden Grane. Near to the main road a community alehouse was established called *Catcham Inn*. Eventually the premises were enlarged and became the *Turks Head Inn. Further up the road another smaller group of dwellings had formed - Well Croft*, which later became *Barley Fold*.

During the early 19th century, Grimshaw Park was developing on both sides of the Bury Road, as a self confident and independent district - from the top edge of the vacant land called *Town's Moor* (in part the regional gas depot is situated on this site) and up to *Barley Fold*. Fronting this last group of property were four dwellings perched up from the roadside, numbered 79, 81, 83 and 85 Grimshaw Park, called *Cob Castle*. Prior to its demolition in 1986, one of the last occupants - Mrs Ethel Saunders, lived with her late husband Alex, at number 85 - the top end house. She recalls that among the deeds - once held by Thwaites Brewery, there was a record book of accounting concerning the retailing of brandy. Once when Alex was stripping off the old wallpaper for redecorating, they discovered a hatch in the dividing wall of the two ground floor rooms. They also noted a lintelled aperture in the gable-end wall which had been filled in. It was thought that this had been used for passing barrels of brandy through. So evidently this was the original Brandy House from which *Brandy House Brow* gets its name. Mrs Saunders also recalls a reference to the business being transferred to premises at the top of the hill - erected in 1847 according to the inscription on a supporting beam within the roof, - and referred to as *Brandy House,* which comprises two large adjoining Victorian houses, numbered 151 & 153 Grimshaw Park, across the road from the *Stop & Rest Inn*.

Across the road from *Cob Castle*, quite a lengthy row of old brick terraced dwellings had been built extending away to reach *Honey Hole Farm*, called *Kemp St*. It was here that the local poet John Thomas Baron was born in 1823.

An excavation into the hillside above Kemp St began in the latter half of the 19th century by *Whittaker's Brow Brick Works*. They produced not only bricks but earthenware pipes and sanitary ware. A housing association estate now occupies what was the floor of the old quarry.

On the other - (East) side - of Brandy House Brow an older quarry had been founded with access from Haslingden Road, this was the *Matthews Brothers Brick Works*. They also toyed with development of a brick making machine. Midway along a cart-track, from Brandy House Brow to Haslingden Road and the quarry entrance, standing beside the excavation was *Cross Fold Farm*.

Eventually the *Blackburn Yarn Dyers* built the works on the vacant quarry floor in 1923 and the office block utilized the foundation of the old farm house.

Across the road from Matthews Brick Works, on the lower north side of Haslingden Road, was the defunct excavation of *Shorrock* old sand stone quarry, and adjoining it a pottery works had been established, resulting in the construction of a very large bee-hive shaped pottery kiln, which could be seen from many parts of the town. At this time, the road leading up to it from Grimshaw Park, was called *Pot House Lane*. *Easington Walk* was built on part of this site.

Previous to this, the road was called *Toll Bar Lane* from when the Blackburn - Elton Turnpike Trust road was established in 1810. According to the *Blackburn Mail* in 1815 it extended from *The Duke of York Inn*, Darwen St. to *Blundle Moss*, Elton. A Toll Bar House was situated on the V-shaped corner of Haslingden Road and Grimshaw Park. This was closed in 1840 and the site redeveloped with dwellings. The *Spring View Inn* beerhouse was built on the very V-corner with bow shaped lintels at ground and upper floor and bowed windows with specially curved panes of glass. The Toll Bar House was resited at the V-corner of *Haslingden Road* and *Old Bank Lane*, across the road from it the *Observatory Inn* was built.

At the bottom end of Grimshaw Park, when it was still detached from Blackburn by open fields, a workhouse was erected in 1761 at the top end of the Town's Moor. (Another workhouse was situated at Waterloo, Livesey). The thoroughfare, from Grimshaw Park, which led to it and down to Nova Scotia, by the *Weavers Arms* at No. 1, High St, was called *Workhouse Lane.* The old Workhouse closed in 1861 when a larger Union Workhouse was built at *Whinney Edge.* Eventually the institution was developed as *Queens Park Hospital.* It was at the old Workhouse that John Osbaldeston a local inventor, spent his last days as a penniless pauper, having been duped of his revolutionary textile invention by a conniving businessman of the town. Old friends rallied round to subscribe funds to provide a honourable burial, and John Thomas Baron wrote some sympathetic verses of the poor man's demise. When Baron died in 1880, he was buried alongside the grave of John Osbaldeston at St. Stephen's parish church, Tockholes.

Consequently *Workhouse Lane* was renamed *Merchant St.* but as the area had become enveloped with Blackburn, the duplication of many street names in various districts needed to be resolved. Thus *Merchant St.* became *Hutchinson St.* A car sales compound now covers the site of the old Workhouse.

If a dividing line was to be drawn, *Hutchinson St.* would serve the purpose. Below it was Park Place, down to the railway bridge and up to Audley canal bridge. This is where Grimshaw Park began, with the *Prince of Wales Inn,* formerly the *Golden Fleece,* standing at the corner of the former *Cross Street.* The Elim Church stands on what was the other side of *Cross St.* of which some old stone setts can still be seen. On the corner of *Merchant St.* stood the *Good Samaritan Inn. Crossfield Mill* has also gone.

The *Turks Head Inn* - an extended development of the *Catcham Inn,* still stands on the corner of Haslingden Road. It closed in 1933 and was converted into a common lodging house. In its hey-day this was the hub of Grimshaw Park - a popular meeting place for the local sports enthusiasts to congregate. It had a large upper floor assembly room.

Adjoining it is an old stone cottage, where I reside and wrote this chapter. This is the only surviving structure of the *Jack Croft* hamlet - the origin of Grimshaw Park.

Owd Sylvester Hindle - The Grimshaw Park Knocker-up

Benita Moore

He came before the rosy dawn
Beset the tranquil sky;
Stars were still alive and gleaming
As Owd Syl clattered by.
A woollen muffler round his neck,
A chequered cap on head,
A rope around his tattered coat -
He'd rouse folk from their bed.
With roughened hand, he gripped a pole
Fixed on the end with metal;
He'd tap each window loud and clear
Folks weren't allowed to settle.
He'd tap and tap - until a shout
Rang-out both loud and clear:
"Thank-you Syl, be on your way
We're up and ready here."
As one by one, bright lamps were lit
In homes 'neath Pennine hills,
Owd Syl went on his lonely way
A' calling folks to t' mills.
When darkness mellowed, the dawn proclaimed
Syl's work was all but done,
He'd stay his pole, turn craggy face
To greet the rising sun.
Sleep well Owd Syl, lay down yer pole,
You've earned a workman's rest;
Held in affection by all you knew,
For you were one of t'best!

The Blackburn Workhouse 1860-90

John Gavan

In early 19th-Century Blackburn, poverty was abundant, but, as elsewhere in the kingdom, steps had been taken to address the social problems it caused. The town joined a Union with its neighbours to operate the Poor Laws in 1836, using a workhouse built in 1764. This contained a weaving shed and allotments in which paupers could work to earn their keep.

In 1861, the Union Workhouse, near to where Nova Scotia Mill is now, held 306 inmates, of which 51 were insane, 55 were over 70 years old, and 57 were under 10 years. Their average age was 41 years. A report published the previous year told of the unsatisfactory conditions - no blankets and enormous neglect of the inmates.

A new workhouse was badly needed for an ever-growing Union population (75,071 in 1841; 235,545 in 1911). One was built on moorland overlooking the town. It remains today a grim outline which would deter applicants from applying for entry. On its 12-acre site, it cost £30,000 to build using stone quarried locally by able-bodied claimants. The first occupants transferred to it from the old workhouse on 16th January 1864 - a period when the Cotton Famine was making life dreadful for thousands in the town.

The workhouse found employ and lodging for those from the Blackburn Union area and also the many vagrants tramping the country in search of work. It housed children and allowed them to be employed in coal pits likely to permanently injure their health. Conditions in the workhouse were anything but pleasant. For vagrants the morning breakfast was *"skilly"* a thin oatmeal broth flavoured with meat - and bread. The editor of the *"Blackburn Times"* saw the place and the whole system as being iniquitous and wasn't afraid to tell readers - *"Poverty is not a crime"*.

In 1881, the inmates numbered 571. Irish inmates were **increasing** - 8 in 1861, 21 in 1871, and 62 in 1881 - this last figure being 8% of the total.

In 1886, tobacco, snuff and beer were being supplied to the inmates (probably to the staff too, as a *"perk"*). In one quarter,

£2.7s.0½d was spent on beer. At this time the average number of inmates was 450.

In 1896 *"The Guardians"* reported that 100 inmates were daily receiving tobacco, and 52 were receiving snuff to help brighten their lives. The food bought from local suppliers was supplemented with vegetables from the workhouse gardens and by pork from the 75 pigs kept.

"The Guardians" managed the Union Workhouse through the workhouse master and his wife, the matron. They controlled the lives, both physical and spiritual, of the inmates. There is some evidence of effort to improve the lot of pauper children, particularly after 1890. There is evidence too that being in the workhouse infirmary screened inmates from the diseases which killed those outside, and the death rate was below the town's average. However, conditions were far from ideal - in 1895, £5 was spent on killing rats.

The Guardians were responsible for housing *"lunatics"* and in 1881 they constructed a separate building for this purpose. (In 1886 it cost 8s. 2d. a week to maintain a lunatic in Whttingham Asylum). The Asylum at the workhouse could house 250.

In 1894, Mr Tiffin, the master, resigned *"under pressure"*, along with his wife. The Guardians found that he had been cruel and tyrannical and guilty of indecent conduct towards a young nurse. Patients had been allowed to lie in maggoty beds *"with bedsores the size of dinner plates and the depth of a cup, and with vermin eating into them"*. There were too many pot-bellied children because of inadequate diet, and inmates had to wear their stockings and shirts for weeks without change.

Tiffin's departure brought a scandal to light, and also saw some changes for the better for the 800 inmates and 38 staff. Amongst the changes was the provision for a daily inspection by the Guardians, though the under-staffing remained, and doubtless remains to this day in the Workhouse building that is now part of Queen's Park Hospital.

The County Council took over the Guardian's responsibilities in 1929.

The Blackburn Trustee Savings Bank

It's 1831. There's something in the air in Blackburn. It's not the smell of beer brewing, or of cattle being rendered down in a glue factory - its PROSPERITY. King Cotton is reigning, houses and factories are being built all over the town. *"T" canal is fair thrang wi' booatloads of awsooarts"*. There's money being made, and so some enterprising gentlemen have got together and set up their own bank to help bring further prosperity to the town and its people (and themselves of course).

There had been a Savings Bank in the town between 1818 and 1829, and there were other commercial banks too. A Savings Bank operated under a different Act of Parliament than did other banks. They were intended to encourage thrift amongst working people, bringing them prosperity through their own efforts.

Early in 1831, 36 gentlemen applied to His Majesty's Government for permission to start the bank. They included men whose names will for ever be linked with the town name - Bannister Eccles, Thomas and William Hart, William Henry and John Hornby. Of the 36, 14 would be *"trustees"*, the others *"managers"*.

A hall in the Sessions House, King Street, was hired and opened on 3rd September. Business was only done on a Saturday between 5pm and 7pm *"to suit the industrial classes"*. However, in later years, increased business brought longer hours on several days of the week. Brothers John, James and Christopher Parkinson were early holders of office within the Board of Trustees. Christopher's daughter married a Mr Lund, who was a manager employed by the bank. A newspaper report of the period (1860's?) doesn't identify which brother is referred to (Christopher was the most prominent) but it does give a sense of dependability which the bankers successfully sought to achieve ....

"Mr Parkinson had been manager of the Trustee Savings Bank when there arose a rumour that the bank had been "broken". Crowds queued to withdraw. It followed a legal ruling that the bank was not a bank, but an association of trustees. It was publicly announced that, if everyone was paid out, there would still be £6,000 left, as well as the buildings, and that the bank had over half a million pounds deposited in the Bank of England. Parkinson piled

72

2000 sovereigns beind the counter for the public to see. £60,000 was paid out in four days, equal to nearly six months savings."

By 1857, it was realised that new premises were needed. A site in what became Lord Street West was selected. A fine building, with stone columns giving it solidity and grandeur, was designed, built and opened in 1863. A great deal of thought went into the selection of the site, the equivalent of what today would be *"market research"*. The land was bought from Joseph Fielden for £200 - (£1 a square yard). The completed building cost £1834.15s, which was £61.15s more than the estimates, a 3% error.

In the town in this period, indeed through Lancashire, were being felt the effects of the Cotton Famine. A Committee organised financial relief for the thousands of unemployed, and made payments in return for work undertaken. Because of the poverty and privation being endured, there was no pompous official opening. It would have given offence and possibly brought civil disobedience. 31% of the population of Blackburn were receiving relief.

In the bank's first year, £1475 was deposited by the 69 account holders, and only £6.0s.4d was withdrawn. After the first year, its funds totalled £106,000. These funds increased steadily until 1878, when the townfolk held back their labour in a 9-weeks strike and accompanied it with rioting, bloodshed and arson. Compared with the previous year (1877), the deposits were down from £61,400 to £52,200, withdrawals increased from £63,800 to £69,400.

In 1863, the Government established the Post Office Savings Bank, which brought increased competition. Some smaller banks had to close, but the Blackburn Trustee Savings Bank responded by opening for more days each week. Business increased and in fact that year marks the milestone in its future prosperity.

Stock was taken (a good banking term) in 1931, a century after the founding. There had been good times and bad, including four years of war. There had been a huge increase in holdings, in annual turn-over and in the number of accounts (50,348 in 1931). Penny Banks had been introduced in schools, giving young Blackburnians the concepts of thrift, savings and reward. It was felt proper that the bank building could be extended from a 40ft frontage to one of 71ft. 6ins. This created a 30ft. boardroom on the first floor, and gave an extra third of solid mahogany counter.

Steady progress in the hands of a Blackburn worthies Board of Trustees and a thoroughly dependable staff continued. More branches were opened outside the town centre and in surrounding

73

towns to a total of 26, and in 1968 a new bank headquarters was built in Preston New Road. In the previous year, the first cheque books had been issued.

In 1974, the bank was controlled, as it was in the 143 previous years by Blackburn men. Colonel H.C. King-Wilkinson, Douglas and Eric Bancroft and Arnold Jepson were amongst the nine trustees. The affairs were managed by Mr D.J. Smith, assisted by Mr W.R. Slater. However, this state of affairs, with assets totalling £70 million, and with almost 300,000 account holders, came to an end in 1975, when the B.T.S.B. merged with others in Chorley, Preston and Carlisle to become the Lancashire and Cumbria T.S.B.

The final transaction in the book, with its local accountability, had been made. The Preston New Road offices were put up for sale in 1978.

For more on the bank and its officers, read *J.G. Shaw "History of the Blackburn Savings Bank" (1931).*

THE NEW SAVINGS BANK IN 1863.   Drawn by Charles Haworth.

Charles Haworth was a manager of the Savings Bank in 1893 when he made this drawing for the Board. The building was then thirty years old.

74

COST OF THE CORPORATION PARK, BLACKBURN, UP TO THE OPENING DAY, OCTOBER 22ND, 1857.

	£	s.	d.
Area of the Park, full 50 acres, at £65 per acre	£3257	6	3
Interest to July 5th, 1856, £172 1s. 1d. ; compensation to adjoining landowners, £77 5s. 11d.	249	6	0
Boundary walls	1583	7	6
Making roads	4480	17	1
Park Entrance	831	15	6
Gardeners, masons, flaggers, paviors, manual and team labour.....................................	2402	4	2
Inspectors	147	14	0
Surveying	80	8	9
Palisading	727	16	6
Railing and fencing for roads........................	28	6	3
Materials......................................	143	13	7
Rent and Taxes	48	7	3
Legal expenses and stamps	32	8	11
Tools and implements.............................	28	8	1
Conveying water................................	53	12	9
Joiners' work, and plumbing	15	15	10
Manure	72	12	7
Seats, plants, shrubs, seeds, &c....................	327	18	2
Landscape gardener and superintendent	116	9	0
Casual expenses	33	16	7
Manual and team labour on opening week	39	14	10
Total cost to the day of opening........	£14,701	19	7

Deduct from the above outlay the proceeds
of sale of the Recreation grounds on the
Town's Moor, viz. :—

	£	s.	d.			
To the East Lancashire Railway Company...	£951	6	8			
Accumulated Interest to April, 1856........	491	16	9			
To the Blackburn Railway Company........	2070	6	8			
Accumulated Interest to 1st July, 1857.......	1188	9	6			
				4701	19	7

Net cost paid for out of borrowed money...............£10,000   0   0

Blackburn, Centre of Medical Focus

On 1st July 1965, an 18 years-old Blackburn girl was admitted to Park Lee Infectious Diseases Hospital with suspected meningitis. Two days later she was transferred to the Infirmary with respiratory distress. She died on 8th July. The post-mortem revealed she had died from acute poliomylitis. The Medical Officer of Health was informed on 10th July.

In the next few weeks, 109 patients were admitted to hospital with a provisional diagnosis of polio. The majority of these initial cases occurred in the Cedar Street area of the town, and on 3rd August the majority of people in this area were vaccinated. Six days later, a major, borough-wide campaign was started. This mass vaccination of Blackburn's 105,000 population, using *Sabin* vaccine, brought the epidemic to a halt within ten days.

Extensive publicity had certainly brought about the increase in cases admitted to hospital. Media-produced hysteria was such that lorry drivers refused to deliver goods to Blackburn. Seaside landladies would not accept visitors from the town. For several weeks, the Blackburn Rovers home matches were postponed and at the end of that season they were relegated to the Second Division. Some unkind critics suggested the fault lay with the Medical Officer's staff.

Blackburn, previous to the outbreak, had been using *Salk* vaccine to innoculate against polio. It was one of only two authorities in the country still using it. Blackburn's neighbouring authorities had previously started to use the *Sabin* vaccine. Blackburn had a lower-than-national-average acceptance rate from those offered vaccination. These factors undoubtedly contributed to the level of polio in the town, though of those 109 cases it was later established that only 20 could be said to have had polio.

In October that year, another illness hit the town - *"epidemic hysteria"*. It affected mostly young girls over a 12-day period, and it was reported upon in the British Medical Journal (26.11.66) as well as in the national press.

85 girls and a teacher at St. Hilda's Secondary Modern School were admitted to hospital, followed some days later by more. In all, 118 girls were admitted.

In trying to ascertain causes, six specialist laboratories co-operated in tests, and a computer was used in analysing data. The girls had been collapsing after feeling faint with breathing difficulties. A later enquiry showed that there may have been a connection between the collapsing and the fact that those girls had been with several hundred other schoolchildren gathered together for up to 3 hours without sustenance for a visit by Princess Margaret to the cathedral. An element of hysteria added numbers to those *"organically ill"*. There were some malingerers too.

The second epidemic lasted but a few days, and appeared not to have greatly affected the girls.

Report on the Conversion of Privies, Pails and Slop-Water Closets to Water-Closets

Amongst the papers kept in the Blackburn Library's Local Collection is a report, titled as above, prepared by the Borough and Water Engineer, Mr A.T. Gooseman in 1920. It marked an important move towards improved sanitation and social conditions.

He had taken a census of the closets of the town, which had 9,278 pail closets, 2,541 slop water closets, 81 privies and 26,457 fresh water closets, which gave a total of 11,819 pail and slop water closets to be converted to *"the water carriage system"*. 58 of these were connected to farm buildings *"and should remain to be emptied on the land"*. 102 were in the more rural parts of the borough and would be expensive to sewer. 42 of the remaining 11,659 would require sewers, and 495 would require the sewers re-laying or enlarging. This would cost the Corporation £84,042, which would include many grants of £3.15s. payable towards the conversion to anyone requesting it. Nothing was granted for privy conversions.

However, all this expenditure would be over several years and would be off-set by the savings made in not collecting pails and the sale of excreta worth £200 a year. The 102 pails and 27 privies left to collect would cost only £150 a year. He estimated that the extra consumption of water by the new method would be 12 gallons per conversion per day. This would not be felt as a cost to the borough (4 million gallons per day) and made no allowance for it.

When converted, the scheme would save the borough £1,065 a year. The Northern side of the town should be started on first *"as this district entails the greatest carting"*.

The Largest Organette Works In The World - In Blackburn

There are several fields of interest in which Blackburn can claim *"first"* or *"best"*, but none of these claims was publicised as often as the claim by Blackburn businessman Joseph Mark Draper that he owned *"the largest organette works in the world"*. He was right, if only on the ground that it was the ONLY organette works in the world.

Joseph was born in Wigan in 1855. He had a brother, James Bartholomew. The latter was the first to come to Blackburn when he married a local girl in 1873. He was a qualified brass finisher. His brother (Joseph Mark) moved to Blackburn in 1879 after marrying a Halifax girl. He set up as a fine art dealer, employing 4 men. They lived in Lower Audley Street and had a son, Joseph Ernest.

On 1st July 1882, the two brothers applied for Patent No. 3119 *"for improving parts of mechanical instruments such as organs"*. By the following eyar they were advertising "ORGUINETTE MUSIC" for sale at 1½d per foot. Humble enough beginnings. In 1884 James moved house next door to Joseph in Lower Audley Street. Business continued to be good, because in the following year, they ceased to work from their homes and moved into a workshop at 35 Clayton Street, expanding into further rooms as business in their orguinette music rolls increased.

By 1886 the brothers made their first organette. Six years later they boasted of having made 16,000. All the designs played the same 14-note music.

1887 saw a further move to a factory in Salford, and their enterprise was now called *"The British Organette & Organette Music Company"*, showing that there were two strands to the business. Business booming, Joseph moved up in housing terms - to 53 Whalley New Road, and again in 1895 to 20, St Alban's Place.

Although, in 1889 an advert for the company appeared (see *Blackburn & Darwen A Century Ago* by Alan Duckworth, 1989) showing them trading from Salford, they were in fact in a shop in High Street, but two years later they moved into River Street, next to Bonnacord Street. This was *"the largest organette works in the world"*. Here they employed between 20 and 30 men making up to 1000 instruments a month, with 620 music titles on the perforated manilla paper available. Joseph attributed their success to advertising. In 7 months he spent £2000 on advertising. They printed their own catalogues of 40 pages, sending out 200,000 in a six-month period.

The introduction, in 1892, of easy-payment methods was enormously successful - 4 shillings down and four shillings monthly. The organettes cost £1.15s, with some at £1 only, others at £1.10s. Their advertising campaign was described as *"second only to that of Mr Beecham"*.

The company leader, Joseph, died suddenly in 1897 aged 42 years, leaving the business in the hands of his brother until his son, Joseph Ernest, could take on the management. He left £16,369.2s.8d. in his will.

By 1901, the company, still advertising heavily, was making standard musical instruments, phonographs and gramophones, but young Ernest had interests outside the world of musical instruments. He guided things towards poultry appliances such as incubators, and opened shops in Audley Range and Accrington.

The company folded in 1935 when Ernest was 58 years old. He died a batchelor in 1940, leaving £10,966.12s.

Draper's success was a mixture of technology and advertising, providing what a music-hungry world wanted. However, a body of opinion has it that he wasn't as straight-forward as he appeared. It is almost certain that he *"borrowed"*, without paying for (?) designs for his products, from those of an American organ builder called John McTammany. No record of a licence to produce the American's designs in this country has been found.

However, it cannot be denied, that, for some years at least, Blackburn did house the largest organette works in the world. Draper may well have been right when he said that he not only worked up a business, he established a new industry. He was an organ builder who blew his own trumpet.

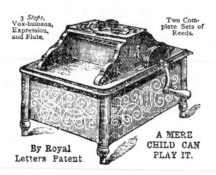

3 *Stops*, Vox-humana, Expression, and Flute.

Two Complete Sets of Reeds.

A MERE CHILD CAN PLAY IT.

By Royal Letters Patent.

There's been a White Bull Hotel on this site since the 1600's. The one shown was built in 1852. The entrance to the underground toilets is seen in the bottom right corner, but pride of place goes to the ornate four-sided tramway standard with the drinking fountain at its base.

(Photo loaned by Stephen Owens)

Thomas Bolton rivalled the Co-ops in feeding and supplying Blackburn. His main shop and head office was in Dickens Street, next to Audley Hall Mills and there were 19 other branches in the town. Customers received *"divi"* for each pound spent. This photo shows a miniature shop which was probably made for one of Blackburn's annual trade processions. It was taken on Billinge Avenue at the junction with Gorse Road.

(Photo loaned by Stephen Owens)

This shot was taken about 1907 and is a marvellous record of town centre life as it was when there were very few motor cars, and the lurries (as it was spelled) were horse-drawn. In the distance can be seen the Theatre Royal.
(Photo loaned by Stephen Owens)

A crowd estimated at being in excess of 200,000 attended the ceremony when H.R.H. Princess Louise came to Blackburn on Saturday, 30th September 1905 to unveil the statue erected to the memory of her late mother, Queen Victoria. It has been the venue for thousands of arranged meetings of Blackburn couples since then. The old lady has seen some sights on the Boulevard since 1905.
(Photo loaned by Stephen Owens)

A late-1950's panorama of The Boulevard. Spot the adverts for locally-made Tizer, Veget bread and O.B.J. beer. Dutton's brewery overlooks the fine offices of the Northern Daily Telegraph. Today the Adelphi Hotel looks out at a scene far different yet still recognisable.

(Photo loaned by Blackburn District Librarian)

Another view of The Boulevard taken in the early 1950's, when few workers had motor cars. The Corporation buses would be full to capacity, with men standing downstairs (they would give their seats to ladies even after a hard day's work in the mills or factories). The buses were in the olive green and cream Corporation livery. Note that the flat cap is still favourite amongst the men.

(Photo loaned by Blackburn District Librarian)

This postcard view bears a postmark of 1913 and shows a traffic-free road where the tramlines are the only worry for cyclists. The Corporation Park gateway is fondly recalled by many exiled Blackburnians.

Station Square is the proper name for The Boulevard, where Blackburners promenaded before it became a 'bus station. This photo was taken about 1910. Take note that Gladstone's statue has not yet been moved to Blakey Moor, that there are trams and horse-drawn hackneys but no motors, and that boaters and flat caps gave clues to one's age or social standing.

It seemed that there was a shop on every corner in the days before supermarkets. Mr Leach had his shop at the corner of Moss Street and Napier Street. Here he stands about 1938. He's probably just put the finishing touches to the whitewash lettering telling of the arrival of the Danish butter.

(Photo loaned by Stephen Owens)

The management and staff of Kirk & Company, Shuttle & Bobbin Manufacturers of Cob Wall Works, Whalley Old Road prepare to set off on their annual trip about 1910. Blackburn made shuttles for the world at this time. How many bare heads can you spot?

(Photo loaned by Stephen Owens)

Taken around the time of the first World War, this photo shows a mobile
advertisement passing the Higher Elementary School on Blakey Moor.
What pleasure there was for little lads to help their mother on washdays
by showing their strength at mangling. The poster on the cart reads
"DELIVERED AT YOUR HOME FOR ONE SHILLING WEEKLY.
JACKSON'S STORES, 56 KING STREET, BLACKBURN".

(Photo loaned by Stephen Owens)

King William Street as it was about 1950 before the redevelopment of the
early '60's. The Market Hall with its adjoining Fish Market and uncovered
market area occupied what is now the shopping precinct and British Home
Stores.

(Photo loaned by Stephen Owens)

The name of Elizabeth Dodds is to be seen (in part) over the door, but Annie Preston, who took over the shop about 1927 has her name proudly displayed in the window. Her shop was located at 48, Redlam. Today the building remains but the window and the bay above have been replaced and it is a terraced house. The well-stocked shop must have been successful as it employed two people, shown here in their shopkeepers' dresses.

(Photo loaned by Stephen Owens)

The 24th of May was Empire Day in the days when Britain had one. It was a day when emphasis was placed on Britain's achievements (in a world in which the maps were coloured red), especially in schools. Perhaps this photo was taken before the arrival of the schoolchildren in the Holy Trinity, Lark Hill, school room. The lady teachers have been busy with the flags and bunting. When the children arrive they'll be singing a special song - *"What is the meaning of Empire Day?"*

A 1922 view of King William Street and the Market Hall clock tower, all 72 feet of it, Blackburn's most famous landmark, destroyed by civic vandalism on 30th December 1964. Robert Peel stands atop the Peel Buildings. Note the golden ball above the clock tower. It rose at noon and descended at 1 p.m., when a gun was sounded at the Town Hall. This went on until 1931. Has the driver of this open-top tourer parked the car or dumped it?

(Photo loaned by Blackburn District Librarian)

The Royal Visit, April 14th 1955. These well-turned out lads and lasses are keeping on the pavement in Victoria Street, which ran from Church Street to Regent Street, passing the back of the Market Hall and the Town Hall. This was probably taken close to Richmond Terrace and St. John's Church.

(Photo loaned by Blackburn District Librarian)

In 1893, there appeared in a directory an advert for G. Grice & Co. of Walpole Street. It was embellished by this illustration of their pipe cleaners. They manufactured tacks and nails, marketing the *"Blackburn"* penny box of nails and *"The Smoker's Combination"*, a most ingenious little article. They claimed to be *"the only firm in the U.K. which produces tacks from the raw material and supplies them finished in boxes at the price of half-penny and one penny"*.

"The house is in telephonic communiction - No. 425"

Blackburn Bobbies

Blackburn was the first town in the county to have *"the new police"* when the Lancashire Constabulary was formed. On 29th February 1840, the Chief Constable, Captain Woodford, issued a written *"general order"* - only his ninth since coming into office - to those men. Within a few days of their appearing on the town's streets, the *"Blackburn Standard"* reported *"The men in their smart blue uniforms have created quite a sensation in the town, for the inhabitants are unused to the sight of such perpendicular individuals pacing up and down the street"*. The order read:-

1. *The Chief Constable directs that the Constables selected to serve in the Division of Lower Blackburn will hold themselves in readiness to proceed to Blackburn on Monday morning next for the purpose of commencing forthwith the duties of their office under the direction of Mr. Superintendent Burke.*

2. *The party will assemble in front of the office at 8 o'clock on Monday the 2nd March with the whole of their clothing and appointments and from thence move off to their stations.*

3. *For the better observance of discipline and in order that there may be some guarantee for an exact performance of all duties required at the hands of the men, the Chief Constable appoints* Constables 101 Andrew MILNE, 111 Robt. McELREE, 70 John SHAW & 222 Robt. MARQUIS *to act as Sergeants until further notice.*

4. *In selecting the above named Constables to perform the very important duty of assisting the Superintendent in exacting from the men the constant and perfect performance of their several duties, the Chief Constable has been guided by the sense he has of the superior knowledge they possess on all points connected with their duty, and he trusts that they will prove by the example they hold forth in their own persons to the men that he has not formed an erroneous estimation of their zeal, intelligence and activity.*

5. *The Chief Constable desires most emphatically to impress upon The Superintendent and the Constables that their chief efforts should be directed to the* **prevention** **of** **crime** *and that the strongest proof they can give of their vigilance, activity and*

discretion will consist in the small amount of crime allowed to be committed in the Division over which they are appointed to watch.

6. *The Constables will make themselves acquainted as quickly as possible with the persons of the Magistrates of their Division and will invariably pay to them the same degree of respect that they will at all times be required to pay to the officers placed in authority over them.*

Before the coming of the county police to Blackburn, the town was effectively policed by one man - the parish constable, though he had men he could call on for assistance, and there were also men employed as night watchmen. This was a continuation of a system of policing which had pertained in England for centuries. The influx of workers into towns, creating population explosions, made it vital that a better system be found, and in 1840 this system arrived in Blackburn. It has been here since.

A hand-written document on Blackburn Library's Local Collection throws light on the old system. It is a statement written by Thomas Perris, the last parish constable to be appointed by the *"Select Vestry"* - the equivalent of the later Watch Committee. He was the successor to John Kay, who died on 18th November 1834. In the opening line, Thomas has mistakenly written 1835 for 1834. The date of the statement is partially illegible, but as he describes himself as *"constable of Blackburn"* it was probably made whilst still in office.

"I have been constable since November 1835. I have no written appointment but the appointment took place at a meeting of the Select Vestry - Mr Fielden attended the meeting. I understand that the Vestry nominated and Mr Fielden approved. An entry of the appointment was made in the Books of the Vestry. I was sworn in by the magistrates but in the course of a few days I was again sworn in at the Court Leet at Clitheroe, held I think in April 1836. I have had no appointment since November 1835, my first appointment being considered permanent, and have not been sworn at the Leet but once, viz in April 1836. My Deputy however has been sworn there every year. In 1836, I think about November, I was sworn again by the magistrates here and again about the same time in 1837. About 12 months ago, I was sworn in at the Quarter Sessions at Preston to act for the Hundred. That was done to enable me to regulate principally the Beer Shops in the neighbouring townships. My assistants were also sworn.

Twice a year, in April and October I attend either by myself or my

Deputy at the Court Leet at Clitheroe and take with me 4 men to act as jurors. The names of the Constables of (space) townships is called - Blackburn amongst others and they answer to their names. No payment is made. Sometimes a printed notice is sent requiring me to attend and to produce 4 men as jurors but most frequently the notice is verbal from Mr Robinson (or Addison?) the steward."

We do know that Perris lived in Chorley at the time of his appointment. He had previously been a constable in Liverpool, where he was born on 27th February, 1803, making him 31 years old when he was appointed in Blackburn.

In the County Record Office, Preston there is a document (Ref QSP 304/80) showing expenses incurred claimed by Perris in the execution of a warrant on Josiah Tipping for a felony committed in Blackburn. Perris travelled to Burton on Trent, Staffordshire (about 100 miles) to take custody of him and return him for trial in 1836.

Jan. 12th	*Coach fare to Manchester*	£0	7s
	Expenses at Manchester	£0	5s
13th	*Coach fare to Uttoxeter Staffordshire*	£1	1s
	For conveyance to Burton-upon-Trent and back	£0	16s
	Expenses at Uttoxeter & Burton	£0	12s 6d
	For maintainance & locking up of prisoner at Uttoxeter	£0	3s
14th	*Coach fare on Self & Prisoner to Manchester*	£2	2s
	Expenses at Manchester	£0	7s 6d
	For Maintainances of Prisoner & Lockup at Manchester	£0	3s
15th	*Coach Fare of Self & Prisoner to Blackburn*	£0	13s
		£6	10s 0d

Crossed out on the document is a line reading "Mr Thomas Perris loss of time in executing the warrant on Joseph Tipping. 4 days at 10/6d per day." Presumably this claim would not be allowed by the town's magistrates.

*   *   *   *

"The History of Blackburn Borough Police 1852 to 1969" by Colin Hey can be seen in the Library's Local Collection.

Wilful Murder

Nine cases of murder in Blackburn between 1852 & 1960

Christine Wilks

Betty Croston, murdered 14th April 1852.

This murder made interesting reading in the *Blackburn Standard* which reported the crime using the dialect of the local people.

"Old" Betty Croston aged 52 had been walking along the canal route from Nova Scotia in the Livesey area with John Cowgill. Both of them had been drinking at the Wheatsheaf in Blackburn and were said to be *"rather tipsy"*. The two had been seen being followed by two men and were later attacked. One of the attackers, Mark Warburton was recognised, Aaron Neville, the other attacker, had been reported to have shouted he would *"— the old woman and kill the old man"*. Numerous local people became involved in the confusion of the misty night. Few clues were found to link these two to the murder other than boot prints around the muddy canal banks: but nothing absolutely conclusive.

Betty had died from drowning having been left by Cowgill who had fled the attack after receiving a bloodied nose. The coroner, John Cort, suggested possibly the strong boots of Warburton had caused the blow to Betty's head rendering her unconscious leading to her subsequent drowning.

Aaron Neville aged 30 from Stakes Hall and Mark Warburton aged 25 from Livesey were found guilty of wilful murder. They were hanged by William Calcraft, public executioner. In those days this meant slow strangulation.

Emily Holland, murdered 28th March 1876.

The most talked about crime of the 19th century by Blackburn people was the atrocious murder of 7 year old Emily Holland. So notorious did this crime become, that a waxworks figure of the murderer was displayed in Madame Tussaud's Chamber of Horrors from 1877 to 1909.

The girl had gone missing after school and although seen by other children around that time in a shop, she could not be traced. Days later the trunk of her body was discovered by Mrs White of

Bastwell Terrace near Lower Ouze Booth Farm, wrapped in newspaper which contained short clippings of human hair. Two bloodhounds, *Morgan* and *Rose* were immediately brought in to search barbers' shops in the area round Moss Street where Emily lived. These dogs played a vital part in tracking down the murderer. Morgan traced a parcel of charred bones and limbs hidden up the chimney of William Fish's shop.

William Fish aged 25 was married with two children and had spent his early childhood in the workhouse. He was hanged at Kirkdale Gaol 14th August 1876 by William Marwood known as *"The Gentleman Hangman"* who had devised his own ropes and table of drops, so that a swift and humane execution took place.

Alice Barnes, murdered 8th November 1892

This crime took place at the gates of Witton Park. Alice Barnes, aged 9, a farmer's daughter from Redlam Farm was carrying out her daily duty of collecting the cows for her father. Near the park gates she was seized by a man who tried to rape her and in an attempt to stop her screaming he forced a handkerchief down her throat so violently that she choked to death. Alice was discovered within 10 minutes of her death, being only fifty yards from the nearest houses off Whalley Road.

Cross Duckworth evaded arrest for more than a week, though a full description of him and his clothing was given by two girls who had seen him and also by a boy who may have disturbed him in the act of violence. Again two dogs were employed from Bromley Cross, *Champion Koodoo* and *Dandy*. The scent, however, had grown cold. In spite of casts made of his boots which did not match exactly and searches made at his home in Primrose Terrace, Bower House Fold the evidence was not conclusive. He was, however, found guilty and hanged by James Billington at Walton Gaol on 3rd January 1893.

Walter Neilson, murdered February 1893

A chemist, Walter Neilson aged 28 years of 40 Whalley Range was found by his assistant Edward John Williams aged 15 years, on the floor of his shop. He had been bludgeoned to death. The length of time that the body had been left, it being stiff and cold on first examination; the lack of a robbery; or any other obvious disturbance of the shop; suggested it had been Williams himself who had committed the murder. A washed pestle used on the victim's head had been found, suggesting that there had been an attempt to cover up the crime. Also Williams had obviously stepped over the body to leave some soda bottles he had collected before he went to get help.

A previous stealing conviction in 1891 and the fact that the boy was serving a two week's notice added to the suspicion of guilt and blame. He was not executed, though he later confessed to the murder. He was released in 1901 after serving 8 years in prison.

Alice Beetham, murdered 20th May 1912

Alice Beetham a girl of 18 became the victim of her lover's frenzy. Both she and her lover Arthur Birkett aged 22 worked at Jubilee Mill where the murder took place.

Alice Beetham had apparently *"thrown him over"* according to local reporting in the Blackburn Times and had insisted that her mother bring her lunch to the mill so as to avoid the chance of meeting Birkett who had been a *"persistent lover"*. Clearly his act was premeditated. He had bought a new razor that morning and whilst Alice had both her arms full carrying a can of weft, Birkett drew her to himself in what looked like a lover's hold and cut her throat. Alice immediately lost consciousness and soon died. Birkett, overcome with grief and horror tried to kill himself in the same way.

Birkett had not been able to get over the fact that Alice had *"chucked"* him and had been extremely *"crammed"* (upset). A memorial cloth was produced in memory of the girl with a poem of Longfellow printed on it. Sympathy lay with Birkett on the day of his execution. All the inhabitants of Riley Street where he lived with his mother and sister, came out to sing *"Abide with me"*.

Helen Chester, murdered 30th June 1935

John Bright Street, Waterfall, Blackburn, was the location of the murder of Helen Chester. A child murder which was never satisfactorily concluded. Helen, aged 3 of John Bright Street had, it was thought, been clubbed to death and her body burnt, leaving stumps where once there had been limbs. The police had suggested that she may have fallen by accident and in a panic the suspected couple had tried to get rid of the body. John Mills a reed maker and his wife Edith both aged 62 years were suspects, living only a few doors away from Helen. John Mills had said to his wife, according to the Blackburn Times *"Don't say a word"*. The crime seemed motiveless. A bloody mallet and a parcel containing remains of the child were found in a neighbour's back yard.

The Mills were charged and found guilty. Blackburn's Almanac later suggested that both were released and the sentence quoshed.

June Anne Devaney, murdered 15th May 1948

The murder of 4 year old June Anne Devaney was a particularly gruesome crime. It was also notable because 46,000 sets of fingerprints from Blackburn's male population over the age of sixteen, were taken in an effort to track down the murderer.

Peter Griffiths aged 22 an ex-Irish Guardsman and his girlfriend had apparently ended their relationship. He proceeded to get drunk. Taking a taxi, he went to Queen's Park Hospital and crept through a window in his stockinged feet, and lifted June Anne out of her cot. His fingerprints were left on a Winchester bottle, as well as footprints and fibres on the polished floor. He violently raped the girl and bashed her head against a wall leaving the body in the grounds of the hospital. The fingerprints and footprints condemned him and he was hanged on 19th November 1948 at Walton Gaol.

The Brewer Street Seige 1958

Harry King, who had been estranged from his wife, entered her house in Brewery Street on 13th December 1958. He carried a shotgun and a seige ensued. Her parents escaped and raised the alarm. Inspector James O'Donnell, who knew King, was asked to try to calm the situation down but as he entered the house he was shot and later died. Another policeman was also injured by King who later shot his wife and tried to kill himself. A gas bomb was used to get King out of the house. He was sentenced to life imprisonment.

The Pawn Shop murder 1960

On 12th February 1960 the body of pawnbroker Frederick Bridgewater Gallagher was found battered to death inside the shop where he worked at Eanam. The main clue which linked the murderer with the victim was a yellow banded wristwatch, which the murderer had taken from the body and tried to sell in South Wales. The scene was said to be quite horrific as the 56 year old Gallagher had fought for his life with the 25 year old Pocze.

Milhaly Pocze was a Hungarian refugee who had escaped from Russia. He was sentenced to death on 1st June 1960 but this was later commuted to life imprisonment.

The Blackburn Poachers: Brutality at Billington

A leaflet, commonly called a broadsheet, was published in 1840 referring to a dark episode in the history of Blackburn. The verses, intended to be sung for they have a one-line chorus, are the work of an anonymous writer and are called *"The Blackburn Poachers"*. A copy is in the Library's Local Collection.

The first verse is:-

Come all you wild and thoughtless youths, and list awhile to me
A dismal tale I will relate that should a warning be.
'Tis of four men from Blackburn town, on killing game intent
Upon the lands of Billington one night a-poaching went.

The verse chorus line is:-

Now all be aware lest you're drawn into a snare.

The song refers to the events of the 20th December 1839 when gamekeeper Thomas Ishwerood, an employee of Mr Hornby, was mortally shot on land near the *"Lord Nelson Inn"*, Billington. His brother and two other men were with him, when they came across four poachers at 1 a.m. Thomas knew two of them - Adam Mercer, known as *"Adam o'Cote's"* and John Crossley. Probably the others were James Parker, known as *"Cronshaw Jim"*, and Joseph Abbott. Arguing turned to fighting, then the gun went off. Thomas fell and was carried to the inn, kept by his father-in-law. He died 90 minutes after being shot.

The constable of Blackburn, Thomas Perris, was notified. It would be one of his last cases before he was replaced (see essay on Blackburn's Bobbies). He searched several houses over the next few days. He knew two of the malefactors, who had all left town.

The Coroner's Inquest was soon opened. The jury's verdict was *"Thomas Isherwood was murdered by Mercer, Crossley and two other persons unknown."*

A week later, Mercer gave himself up to Mr Perris. It appears that Crossley fled to America via Ireland but died in a workhouse 9 months after the incident. He was severely disturbed, so scared he had altered his facial appearance when in Liverpool about to sail.

In 1840, Mercer, who was not proceeded against, was given bail to appear as a witness when the others were to be brought before the court.

There my telling of the story ends, for I have been unable to trace the results of the Lancaster Assizes proceedings. It is a fascinating tale worthy of the attention of someone keen to finalise the story of an early Blackburn murder.

The Blackburn Abduction Case

If there had been a *"tabloid press"* in 1891, it would have been full of a Blackburn-based story which captured the imagination of the nation.

Edmund Haughton Jackson, of Blackburn had been introduced to Miss Emily Hall, daughter of a wealthy Clitheroe solictor at a Sawley picnic in 1881. Six years later, in October 1887, he "out of the blue" popped the question to her whilst on Wilpshire Railway Station. She agreed, despite knowing that her friends, and probably her family, disliked Jackson.

MR. EDMUND HAUGHTON JACKSON.

It was a whirlwind engagement. A week or so later, on 5th November (a night for fireworks, remember) they were married in St. Paul's Church, Blackburn. There wasn't much of a honeymoon, as, on the following day, with his new wife's knowledge and perhaps encouragement, Edmund sailed to seek his (i.e. their) fortune in New Zealand with a Mr Robinson, a Clitheroe friend. Jackson had previously served as a captain in the New Zealand Army, fighting the Maoris.

Letters were exchanged, and in the following March, Edmund noticed that his wife's attitude had changed. She became abusive over the financial arrangements of their marriage. He returned home, arriving back in England in July 1888.

On his arrival in Clitheroe, Emily refused to see him or have anything to do with him. She was under pressure from her family, who disliked Jackson, probably thinking that he had married Emily only for her considerable wealth, and feared he would take her away from them.

A year later, with his conjugal rights still being denied, he applied to the courts for an order restoring those rights. She still refused to see him, so Edmund devised a plan.

On the morning of Sunday, 8th March 1891, Edmund, Dr Robinson of Clitheroe and Dixon Robinson the doctor's son(?) - his New Zealand trip-mate, physically captured Emily from outside Clitheroe parish church, where she was with her mother, bundled her into a carriage and took her to *"West View"*, Rover Street, Blackburn. (Later to be called Wellfield Road), the house of his sister. There she remained for eleven days whilst her relatives laid seige to the house. Edmund denied she was a captive.

Emily's father devised a campaign. He applied to the High Court for a writ of *"habeas corpus"* to force Edmund to bring her to the court *"where she might be set free"*. However, the judge dismissed the application, as he believed Edmund was within his rights. However, an appeal heard the following day overturned the judge's decision, bringing the couple before the court again.

In private, the judges conferred with both parties, as a result of which Emily left the court by the judge's entrance, still *"Mrs Jackson"* but free from her husband's attentions.

Later that month, Edmund and his friends appeared before the packed Clitheroe Police Court to answer charges they had assaulted Emily and her mother. The case was dismissed, with costs of 8 guineas being awarded against the complainants.

In May, there was *"an extra special"* Saturday afternoon production at the Theatre Royal, Blackburn - a play by J. Barker called *"The Abduction of a Wife"*. There were 21 actors for the 4-Act play set in Blackburn, Clitheroe and London.

Edmund died at his Twickenham home in June 1924 aged 84. His wife died aged 54 years in 1898.

Body Snatching in Blackburn

About 1 o'clock in the morning of Friday 28th September 1827, the watchman of Chapel Street, Joshua Howarth, going on his rounds near St Peter's Church, observed two suspicious-looking men standing near the Grammar School. He went to ask their business. They gave evasive answers, so he ordered them off. They moved off and he followed to watch them. Soon they returned towards the Independent Chapel yard, and after five minutes, Joshua heard something fall. He sprang his rattle, which made the two run off with Joshua in pursuit. He soon lost sight of them. Returning to where he had seen them, he met Joseph Eccles who had been roused by the rattle. He asked the watchman to check his house, but all was well. However, close by the chapel wall they found a shovel and two sacks, which contained a body. A further alarm was given. St Peter's church and the chapel were searched. In the latter, a recently-opened grave was found. The body was that of a poor woman called Ann Whiteley, who had drowned in a lodge the previous Saturday.

A few days later William Fletcher was arrested on suspicion of body-snatching and taken before the magistrates in the Sessions Room. Joshua Howarth *"could not swear to him"* (i.e. identify) and he was discharged.

It was likely that the newly-interred body was taken for sale to a surgeon. Were Fletcher and his accomplice Blackburn's Burke and Hare?

Blackburn Steeplechase

Marc Duckworth

The day was a most delightful one, on March 30th 1840, being of a gentle spring breeze of ethereal mildness. All the morning, carts heavily laden with forms, barrels of beer and other creative comforts, were to be seen winding their way to the scene of action, and as early as ten o'clock a move of the populace along the road was perceptible. Between 10.00 a.m. and 1.30 p.m. the whole line of road was one continuous mass of human beings. Thousands upon thousands had congregated on the grounds until there could be no less than 20,000 persons present. Good judges and men who have experience in estimating numbers say 30,000 people were there. It is true that Blackburn and all the towns and villages around were in a manner depopulated, because they went to the races. A denser crowd than that lined the hillside on the right hand side of the road. The race was situated less than 3 miles from Blackburn on the road to Whalley. It was a short distance beyond the Bull's Head, and the view from the fields near the starting-post and stand was of the finest features of Ribblesdale. The town and castle of Clitheroe could be seen in the distance. It was chiefly grass land, practicable fences, all of them affording a fair trial of a horse's powers, with the exception of three. There were no artificial stonewalls to break the backs of horses and the necks of riders. This was a good thing and planners today could learn from the example of Blackburn Steeplechase. The average bet was a shilling, which was a lot of money in those days.

The gentry were separate from the working class. They had their own enclosure, the working class were not allowed anywhere near. Most of the crowd that came to watch were standing near the starting post. The biggest crowd of Blackburn Steeplechase was March 29th 1844 which was to be the last meeting, 50,000 people were around the stand, independent of multitudes of people who took up a place on the hillsides to get a better view of the ground.

The first race was at 2.00 p.m., with six runners and the prize a sweepstakes of fifteen sovereigns each, with 100 sovereigns added. All six runners had a weight of 12 stone each. There were 50 leaps in all. In the first race the horse *Valentine* won with flying colours. *Sir William* came second, *Antonio* was third. It took about 11 minutes for the winner to complete the course.

In the second race of the day *Little Peter* won by several lengths. *Merry Lad* was second and *Defence* was third. Six horses ran.

The third race was for a sweepstakes of five pounds each paid by four Blackburn gentlemen. There were four horses in the race - *Miss Fanny, George, Paddy* and *Jack*. The last race of the day proved to be the most exciting of all. *Miss Fanny* took the lead at the start, followed pretty close by *Jack* and George. At this time *George* was 30 yards behind but the two leading horses passed on the wrong side of the flag staff, and had to turn back. *Miss Fanny* lost no time from her mistake and gained amazingly on *George*, coming a few fields from home. But her exertions had pumped the wind out of her. She couldn't quite get her nose in front. Neck and neck the two came flying over the fences together. A most punishing struggle along the turf ensued, *George* winning by half a neck. *Miss Fanny* came second, followed by *Jack*, last was *Paddy*.

When the sports day terminated, a most extraordinary scene occurred. The immense mass of people, who had arrived at different periods in a space of several hours, all wanted to set off at the same time. Not just the gates and gaps out of the fields, but the road itself was for a while blocked by thousands. There were no accidents (apart from a boy falling from a tree, injuring his arm) to mar a most splendid occasion at the races. It was to last 4 years and never be forgotten.

Blackburn Olympic

Harry Berry

At a time when Jack Walker's millions have raised the profile of Blackburn Rovers in the public eye, and the talk is that the silverware from a major trophy may at last be destined for Ewood Park it is perhaps timely to recall the first time a national trophy returned to Blackburn. The first club to break the domination of the South-East by winning the English Cup (in 1883) was not the Rovers but *"Blackburn Olympic"*. The club was consigned to a pauper's grave more than a century ago. It rose from obscurity, struggled gloriously against overwhelming odds and died unlamented. Yet in one season the players who were plucked from local life spearheaded the vanguard that changed forever the face of English football. Until that moment the cup had always been handed tō representatives of the aristocracy, students from Oxbridge, military men from the elite regiments or men who were just simply well connected. In 1883 a Blackburn plumber went up to receive the cup, leading his team of four cotton mill workers, two iron foundry hands, a picture framer, clerk, publican and dentist.

The Olympic were born in 1877, perhaps out of frustration. Football had been played in the Blackburn area from 1865, spread by the influence of people educated at the Southern public schools and introduced gradually to the working class. One of the men responsible locally for this pioneering work was the famed *"Monkey"* Hornby, whose family owned mills in the area. Hornby was to play cricket for Lancashire and England, rugby for the national side and was a noted competitor at local athletic events. From the time he challenged the young men in his father's mills to take up the sport he was actively involved in organising games and running his own team. He called it the *"Rovers"* and it consisted of some of the town's leading figures. Sir Harry Hornby occasionally took part and so did Joseph Law, a local bookseller who later had a fashionable book shop in Charing Cross Road. When John Lewis and Arthur Constantine called the historic meeting in the St Leger Hotel in 1875 that resulted in the formation of the current Rovers they were in reality only continuing the evolution Hornby had commenced.

Within two years the Rovers threatened to dominate the football scene in Blackburn. Other clubs such as "Livesey United" and

"Cob Wall" had preceded them but the Rovers had the ambition and the patronage of the wealthy. The remainder of the local teams viewed them with suspicion. Two, "Black Star" and "James Street", decided to do something about it. They began talks about amalgamating and in 1878 sent out their first combined team. Having been elected both captain and treasurer, James Edmondson was allowed to select a name. He chose the title "Olympic".

The entire episode might have simply been the posturing of envious little men if fate had not decreed that the Olympic inherited some rare football talent. Two men shone. Thomas Gibson worked in a foundry and played wing half with all the steel that manual labour had honed into his body. He was only 5 feet 4 inches tall but was feared throughout the game. A quiet, retiring man he suffered for these qualities. Unquestionably the best wing half in the town, he never received international recognition which would have meant little if the national selection was not the Rovers' Fred Hargreaves. Even smaller than Gibson was Joe Beverley, a right wing or centre forward, who later did gain international honours. By that time he was a right back and playing in the blue and white halves of the Rovers.

Initially the club played against regiments of foot soldiers from Preston Barracks and local clubs. In their first season they won the cup for local teams donated by Livesey United and the following year when the Blackburn Football Association took over the organisation of the competition they defended it. This would have made them cock of the town midden if the Rovers had not deemed such a trial of superiority below their dignity. By refusing to enter they left local issues unresolved but on February 15th 1879 the teams finally took to the field. The lordly Rovers slunk off beaten by three goals to one. The Rovers were never as complacent again and commenced a policy from which only the fittest could survive.

That was never likely to be the Olympic. They were always hard pushed financially, existing mainly because of the benevolence of Sidney Yates of the local iron foundry W. & J. Yates. Their experiences with their ground were heartbreaking. Initially they rented the cricket field at Hole 'ith Wall which was so narrow that Beverley, who was a long throw expert, could hurl the ball out of play on the opposite side. They spent a hard earned £100 in widening it only to find that the ground was commandeered for the clay under it which was needed for making bricks. An ill-fated spell at Pleckgate cost them the allegiance of fans who deserted to the more centrally placed Rovers in Leamington Road. To remedy this they moved back to Hole 'ith Wall onto the ground of the defunct

King's Own. This pitch drained so badly that one writer remarked *"anything worse would be called a duck pond"*. In 1884 their grandstand blew away.

As compensation, they discovered a succession of brilliant natural footballers. They were also innovative. When the rest of the world played a 2-2-6 formation the Olympic were the first to switch to 2-3-5. They also tested a system that utilised Beverley as the world's first *"libero"*, sweeping up behind his defence. In 1880 they entered for the English Cup for the first time and were drawn to the mighty *"Sheffield Association"*. Trailing by four goals and outclassed they produced a fight back of heroic proportions that did not quite produce an equaliser but left the home side grateful to the woodwork. Heroic failures seldom have important consequences but this may have achieved more than most for it brought them to the notice of the footballing elite in Sheffield, where the game was stronger than in most cities. Eighteen months later the teams returned for a fixture with "Heeley" and the meeting that was to shape destiny.

Jack Hunter was a gnarled veteran who played centre half for Heeley and had done for England. He was a legend in the Yorkshire game but was in the process of being hounded out of it by Pierce Dix, a local official and referee. A select side had been gathered in the city that played games in theatrical garb. They were known as the "Zulus" and Dix had unearthed the fact that they were transgressing the rules on amateurism by paying expenses. Hunter knew well that he faced suspension or heavy fines and that his opponent would not be appeased. Anxious to escape the city he offered his services to the Olympic as unofficial coach if they could meet his financial requirements. These consisted only of obtaining him the licenseeship of a public house so that he would have a salubrious means of living. This the Olympic could stretch to, and so Hunter crossed the Pennines.

He proved to be everything he had represented himself to be. Taking charge of the club completely he organised and directed on the field. Nominally a centre half, he was to fill in in any position and thanks to his knowledge the club prospered. When he decided that 33 goals in six games still underlined a lack of fire power, the committee allowed him to visit Salford and bring back George Wilson, a colleague from Sheffield who had been forced to leave because of the Zulu scandal. To engage Wilson employment had to be found for him as a clerk but the Olympic still had the benefit of one or two supporters with influence in the town. Of course the Rovers had even more influence and Wilson's arrival was offset by the loss of Beverley, the first of many to learn his game with the

Olympic and graduate to fame with the Rovers. Initially the joke was on Beverley. Having thrown in his hand with the Rovers because of the possibility of assisting them in progressing beyond the losing finalists position they had reached in 1882, he could only watch with envy as his old team mates beat the Rovers in the race to lift the cup.

The English Cup was played in zones so the Olympic were only too aware that in all probability they would have to defeat the Rovers. They were prepared having defeated them in the final of the East Lancashire Charity Cup. Fate was kind to Olympic. The Rovers fell to another bitter rival "Darwen", who then obligingly lost to "Church". By beating "Padiham", "Accrington", "Lower Darwen" and "Church" the Olympic reached the quarter finals. From then on the zoning ended but the next opponents were still familiar. *"The Welsh Druids"* had previously discomforted them with robust play. This time the Olympic were prepared and the tiny Blackburn men, who averaged only 5'6" per man, hit their beefy opponents like a whirlwind and ran out winners by three goals.

The semi-final played at Whalley Range pitted them against the game's elite in the shape of the *"Old Carthusians"*. On a bitterly cold day no-one was amused that the kick off was delayed because no ball had been provided and the projecting ends had to be sawn from the crossbar. Snow melting on a heavy pitch was deemed to favour the more athletically proven old boys but the Olympic won by four goals. For the final at Kennington Oval the team again elected to take the air at Blackpool before the crucial match.

Hunter had worked wonders with the team, but the smart money was on their opponents, the *"Old Etonians"*. They had outlasted the Rovers the previous year and were totally experienced in games of this standing. Apart from Hunter, no-one, not even the veteran Gibson, had experienced similar situations. Jim Ward was just eighteen, and Tom Dewhurst was a year older. The inside forwards, Matthews and Yates had combined together only the previous year. Jimmy Costley had been at the club for only a matter of weeks. However the team had character and ability. The waif-like Thomas Hacking had become arguably the finest goalkeeper in the game. Matthews, who became a Presbyterian minister in Canada, had developed into a complete inside forward and Wilson led the line with dash.

After twenty-three minutes the Etonians took the lead through Chevallier. The pundits sat back. The score certainly transformed the game though not as predicted. After scoring, the Southerners ran out of steam and the Olympic poured forward. They struck the post and the crossbar and twenty minutes into the second half struck gold. In the first half the robust Etonian winger Dunn had clashed with young Ward and shaken him badly but in doing so he chose a bad enemy. Ward was superbly competitive in everything he did. Jumping, running, wrestling, he took on anybody at any sport for money or a dare. When Dunn shaped up to repeat his treatment on him Ward was ready, met him in a bone shaking challenge and watched with some satisfaction as his opponent limped off. Within a minute, Matthews had equalised and the tide was flowing one way. How the old boys held out until full time was a miracle but they were studded with internationals and Lord Kinnaird organised the resistance. Indeed in the very last minute his eminence almost set up Macauley to steal the game. His shot would have beaten any goalkeeper in the land, but not Hacking who threw himself uncoventionally feet first and hacked the ball to safety.

The Etonians had no need to consent to extra time, especially as they were a man short but their honour would not permit withdrawal. Within a minute they were punished for such glorious traditions when little Costley who would have been omitted in favour of Parker if the weather had been fine, cut in from the wing and scored the winning goal. The festivities were riotous. The town's MPs, Coddington and Briggs entertained them in London. In Blackburn the station was jammed as the public awaited the train from Wigan. The players were carried shoulder high to the wagonettes that ferried them around town.

Within six years the Olympic would be history, condemned to a pauper's grave and remembered only by the greatest Olympian of them all, Thomas Gibson. The reasons were obvious. The Rovers immediately countered by winning the cup three years in succession, sweeping the town's support with them. The club's patron Mr. Yates declined in health and without his influence they were unable to offer the players sufficient inducement to stay. Preston had George Wilson behind the bar of a town centre public house before the next season started. When Wilson got married an acerbic Olympic official was heard to enquire whether North End had provided the wife as well as the pub. The Rovers, Burnley and Accrington joined Preston in preying on Olympic's talent. The club secretary, William Bramham, pitted all his wiles in an unavailing fight to keep players. He had the team on the field within two days of the draw for the first round of the English Cup, in order to cup tie them for the season. Often when he heard rumours of the Rovers being on the prowl he would whisk stars away to Blackpool for the weekend. He once hid Dewhurst down a coal mine to escape such attentions. However, money ran out and when the players were placed on half wages the inevitable happened. Ward, *"El Dorado"* Costley and Beverley, who had returned, left the Rovers. Dewhurst went to Halliwell, Yates had already joined Accrington. Players had become disillusioned. Hacking retired to concentrate on dentistry. His replacement Leigh had less dedication. He once turned up without his shorts and played a terrible game trying to keep his long trousers from becoming muddy. Ward forgot his boots and played in his clogs until the opposition objected.

Standards declined. They were not elected to the newly formed Football League. Jack Hunter was asked to confine his acquisitions to the junior clubs in town. When they signed their first ever Scot, McLeod of Cowlairs, they were unable to pay his wages within a month and lost a fine player. They made a brave face of not being elected to the elite and beat clubs as capable as Everton, Distillery and Bury but as the season progressed and the players left the defeats became embarrassing. Sides like Irwell Springs, Farnworth Star and Hurst thrashed them. The following season they did not even enter for the English Cup. Three weeks later they were extinct, their ground passing to the Railway Clerks. It provoked a brief flurry of action and a meeting was called to revive the team. The only man of substance to turn up was Thomas Gibson. The meeting allowed the club to pass into history.

This was a club born to live for the one glorious hour. Fate conspired against them throughout their history. Only one man, Jim Ward, wore the international shirt when with the club, although some Olympians played for their country. Thomas Hacking missed selection because he was injured when knocked from a train as he alighted at the station. Tom Dewhurst was picked and then de-selected because he had intervened when his team-mate Costley was attacked by an opponent. Defending the English Cup they reached the semi-final where they lost to the Scottish club *Queens Park,* amid claims that the crowd cost them the game. Indeed they always contended that a vital goal came from a defence splitting pass made by a spectator and another was deflected in from the boots of a policeman. When the Rovers took the cup for the third consecutive time the Olympic had been expelled from the tournament as punishment for playing a player in goal who had already cup tied, even though this fact was not known to the club. That same player, Jack Southworth, went on to become a legendary centre forward with the Rovers, Everton and England. Fate was seldom kind to *Blackburn Olympic.*

The Conquering Heroes: East Lancs' First Championship - 1919

Gerry Wolstenholme

On 23 July 1863 an eleven of the 2nd Lancashire Rifle Volunteers defeated Blackburn Cricket Club on the latter's ground at Daisyfield. The victors then decided to form a private club of their own. It was to be a prestigious club and applications for membership would be strictly scrutinised, so much so that two black balls could be used by the committee to veto an application to join. Because of this the club gained the nickname of the *'Cuff and Collar Brigade'*. But by the end of September of that year the East Lancashire Cricket Club was established, with its ground at Alexandra Meadows, then leased by a Major Lund.

1864 saw the club's first season. With two professionals, Yorkshireman Luke Greenwood and Joseph Kay, and a select membership of 200 they arranged fixtures with Preston, Great Harwood, Cheetham Hill, Clayton-le-Moors, Church, Bolton, and Stonyhurst. In 1892 the formation of the Lancashire League, out of the old North-East Lancashire League, brought together the East Lancashire townships and it was then that their rivalry, that continues to this day, started in earnest. And it was also then that a brass band would greet a championship side on the outskirts of town with the rendition of *'See the Conquering Hero'*; a tradition, unfortunately, long since past.

East Lancashire were runners-up in the league in 1896, (a point behind Nelson), 1901, (with a then-record £365 gate receipts), 1913 and 1916. But in 1919 after competitive league cricket had been suspended for two years, they won their first title. And a close run contest it was as they pipped Nelson by a single point, the difference coming in the very last game of the season.

The club had lost members in World War I but the committee felt that cricket should be played despite the difficulty in getting a team. Vic Norbury, who had appeared in first-class cricket for Hampshire and was to appear in eight games for Lancashire in 1919, was re-engaged as professional and it was around his all round performances, (974 runs at 41.62 and 98 wickets at 10.99), together with those of the leading amateurs Josiah Coulthurst, (101 wickets at 9.78), and Dawson, (879 runs at 39.95), that the championship was won.

An inauspicious start was made. In the first game at home to Nelson, East Lancs, bowled out for a paltry 84, were defeated by two wickets. A draw followed against Todmorden before three successive victories moved them up the table. Rawtenstall, Lowerhouse and Enfield were defeated with Norbury capturing 5-15 and 6-31 in the first two games and Coulthurst 6-36 in the third.

The return match against Rawtenstall was drawn and then Todmorden, Church, Lowerhouse and Burnley were all beaten in turn. Norbury made 96 against Lowerhouse but it was the victory over Todmorden that moved them into second place in the table behind the all-conquering Nelson. A set-back away to Haslingden, for whom Riley took 7-40, followed but then came eight straight wins. The visit of Haslingden brought record gate receipts of £142 but it was the sixth game against Rishton that took them to the top of the table for the first time. Norbury and Coulthurst did most of the damage with the ball and then against Colne, Norbury, (116), and Dawson, (107), put on an unbroken 223 for the second wicket. Norbury then bowled Colne out with 6-50.

A draw with Burnley while Nelson were winning meant that the Seedhill club re-joined them at the top of the table. And then back-to-back fixtures with Bacup, a win and a defeat, pushed East Lancs down to second. Accrington were defeated twice at the end of August, the home fixture being won by one wicket where the batsmen, Coulthurst and Stones, were carried off by spectators amidst scenes of great enthusiasm as the team moved back to joint top of the league. Ironically the penultimate match was against Nelson at Seedhill and a draw saw the two clubs go into the last match of the season neck and neck.

And so to the last game of the season. Nelson were playing Ramsbottom while East Lancs were at home to Colne and both were expected to win. A play-off had therefore been provisionally arranged for the following week. But it was not needed, as, much to everyone's surprise, Nelson were beaten by Ramsbottom and East Lancs defeated Colne with Norbury contributing 7-39 and 63 not out to leave East Lancs outright champions.

As events unfurled, the League secretary, William Barlow, had to rush the cup by car from Ramsbottom. In the true spirit of sportsmanship, Mr Briggs, of the Nelson club, travelled with

Barlow to offer his congratulations to the new champions.

The large crowd at Alexandra Meadows was ecstatic, none more so than Thomas Eastwood who was in his 39th year as secretary of the club. The League secretary presented the cup to Harry Emmett, the East Lancs' captain, and said that at the end of the reconstruction year he was glad East Lancs, who had the distinction of finishing second to Nelson in 1896, had now been successful in winning the cup. He offered his congratulations along with those of Mr Briggs.

The crowd cheered when Emmett received the cup and called for all the players to appear on the balcony. Emmett said that it was a great day in the history of his club and that although they had not expected winning the trophy that day, he was confident of winning it in the play-off with Nelson the following week. He added that it was their intention to retain the cup in Blackburn. James Campbell, the East Lancs' chairman, added his congratulations and appreciation of the team's success.

Unfortunately East Lancs did not retain the trophy the following season and did not win it again until 1942. Since then they have won the Lancashire League title on 11 occasions. But none of these triumphs brought quite the same euphoria as that very first championship way back in 1919 when the *'Cuff and Collar Brigade'* were feted by the brass band booming out the victory anthem *'See the Conquering Hero'.*

BOYLE'S JAP NUGGETS.

"The Best on Earth."

Boyle's
Invalid
Toffee.

Boyle's
Treacle
Toffee.

Boyle's
Real
Hum-
bugs,
$2\frac{1}{2}$d.
per qr.

JAMES BOYLE AND COMPANY, LIMITED.

7, RAILWAY ROAD,

BLACKBURN.

86 Years on the Spot.

BRANCHES :—

DARWEN STREET, BLACKBURN.   MARKET STREET, DARWEN.
EXCHANGE, BLACKBURN.   PROMENADE, BLACKPOOL.

Working Men Botanists of Blackburn

Stanley Miller

Towards the end of the 18th Century, and in the early years of the 19th, there developed among the working men of Lancashire an intense interest in the study of plants, which is astonishing in view of the long hours they worked, and the limited opportunities for study. In the words of the natural history writer for the Victoria County History of Lancashire *"A group of self-taught naturalists, who for the most part, born in quite humble circumstances, without education, and denied all the assistances to self-education now so abundant in our large towns... their scant leisure was employed in assiduous collecting and expeditions on foot."*

Mrs. Gaskell comments on the botanists in Mary Barton: *"Scattered all over the manufacturing districts of Lancashire are botanists who know the name of every plant within a day's walk from their dwellings".*

One of the most celebrated of the Blackburn working men naturalists, Thomas Nuttall, was born at Long Preston in North Yorkshire on January 5th, 1786. He spent his school days at Blackburn, and on becoming apprenticed to the printing trade began his work of studying the local flora of the hills and valleys around the town. In 1807, Thomas Nuttall emigrated to the United States, settling in Philadelphia, which became a base for his explorations of the North American continent. He undertook several journeys of over 1,000 miles, and visited almost all the States of the Union. No one made more botanical discoveries than Thomas Nuttall. In 1813, he received the premier award for field naturalists, Fellowship of the Linnaean Society. On receiving a bequest of an estate *"Nutgrove"* from a relative in 1842, Thomas Nuttall returned to his native Lancashire, to the town of St. Helens, where he died on 10th September, 1859.

George Ward was a handloom weaver born in 1791 at Witton, and followed this calling for many years before becoming a *"loomer"*. Looming was a trade taken up by many former handloom weavers on the decline of their own craft. It was a skilled and laborious task, which entailed taking the warp threads from the weaver's beam, threading them through the healds and reeds, and getting the power loom ready for the weaver.

In his spare time, George Ward walked through the countryside all round Blackburn observing the plant life. He was a familiar figure to ramblers in the Ribble Valley. Several of his records are published in Thomas Dobson's book on the Ribble Valley, "Rambles by the Ribble". He was interested in the medical properties of the plants, and may have owned a copy of "The New Herbal", published in Blackburn in 1808. George Ward made the first attempt at compiling a Flora of Blackburn, but this remained in manuscript. In later life, George moved to Billinge End, where he died on July 23rd, 1880.

The next botanist to work in Blackburn was a boot and shoe maker of Church Street, who came to the town about 1816. Thomas Townley was regarded as leader of the local botanists, as he had a good botanical library, and organised the first local Botanical Society, which met at the Jolly Dragoon Inn at Moulden near Feniscowles, and was named the Moulden Water Botanical Society. By comparing notes, and exchanging plants, the members were encouraged to develop their knowledge of plants and the local flora, while the plants looked better "viewed through a glass". the book collection was available to help with problems of identification.

In September 1819, the members of the Moulden Water Society met their colleagues from Preston, Bolton, Wigan and Chorley at the White Horse Inn in Chorley, where 700 botanical specimens and herbs were put on display. Thomas Townley did not collect plants, as he was a skilled water colourist, and perferred his paintings to dried and shrivelled leaves. He moved to Bolton in 1824, and from there to Manchester, where he died in September 1857.

While residing in Blackburn, Thomas Townley trained the fourth of the early band of naturalists. George Crozier was born in Great Eccleston near Blackpool and came to Blackburn in 1815, when he opened a saddler's shop in Darwen Street. He was a Nonconformist, and attended Chapel Street Independent Chapel, where his son Robert and daughter Hannah were baptised. His son Robert showed an early aptitude for painting, and was encouraged in this by Thomas Townley, who was thus the mentor for both father and son. The former became a remarkable field naturalist, the latter a successful portrait painter. George Crozier moved to Bolton about 1822, and finally settled in Manchester in 1831, where Thomas Townley followed him to Peel Street, Hulme. George

Crozier's saddler's shop was on Shude Hill, and was a meeting place for his fellow enthusiasts. He quickly became an authority on the plants of his adopted town, but died before his projected *"Flora"* was completed. At his funeral on 24th April, 1847, most of the local botanists were in attendance.

The removal of the two principal members of the Moulden Water Society brought about its speedy demise, and local botanical activity shifted to Accrington. In 1847 there were enough botanists to organise a botanical ramble with naturalists from Bury, Salford and Manchester on the occasion of the arrival of the first train from Bury to Accrington. However, the Accrington Society lapsed soon afterwards, and when the Accrington Natural History Society was formed in 1855, the majority of the members were drawn from the middle and professional classes. Similarly, the Blackburn Field Naturalists Club of 1875 was composed of professional people.

The Victoria County History comments on this change: *"The present local students belong to a somewhat different social order. With better education, and a wider grasp of the scope of biology, their contributions are more likely to survive than was the case with an older generation."* The Todmorden naturalist Abraham Stansfield had a different explanation: *"The silly craze for violent athletics affected all the quiet studies. Everybody seemed to have gone made on football ... Time was when men could find pleasure in roaming the countryside in search of the things of nature, but no longer."*

The Jews of Blackburn

Eddie Conway

In the thirty or so years preceding the Great War close to three million Jews emigrated from East Europe to escape from poverty, persecution and social discrimination. A comparative small number, pioneering idealists, journeyed south to fulfil a religious obligation by settling in the promised land of Palestine. The overwhelming majority, more pragmatic, travelled west to a land of promise - the United States.

Whether by design, default or sheer fortune not all completed this arduous journey and some quarter of a million Jews journeyed no further west than the United Kingdom. Suddenly towns that had little contact with Jews before the 1880's became hosts to small communities. One such town was Blackburn.

Given these factors, Blackburn at the turn of the century offered opportunities for these immigrants to start a new life and create a new community. Blackburn typified an industrial town which had grown as a result of the industrial revolution and in the course of a hundred years up to 1909 had expanded from a small market town into the largest town of north-east Lancashire. Its municipal buildings and status reflected its prosperity, a factor with an undoubted appeal for a newly-arrived immigrant searching to establish a living. It was within easy rail reach of Manchester, a city with a large Jewish community and besides its own large market there were within ten miles radius two large towns, Preston and Burnley, and several smaller mill towns, all possessing busy markets.

Therefore, as a centre of a network of markets Blackburn had a strong appeal for the Jewish *"market stander"*. Its size and position meant it possessed a thriving shopping centre with a considerable burgeoning tailoring trade satisfying local middle-class demand and so presenting opportunities for the traditional Jewish tailor. These three factors, a prosperous regional centre, a large market centre in a network with smaller networks and its proximity to Manchester combined to make Blackburn an attractive proposition for Jews whose traditional trades were

116

tailoring, glazing, cabinet making, picture framing, shopkeeping, credit drapery and market trading.

Although isolated Jews lived in the town before the 1880's, its Jewish population grew so that by the spring of 1893 an appeal for funds to establish a synagogue appeared in the *"Jewish Chronicle"* the major Jewish weekly. This appeal claimed that over twenty families lived in the town and several more in its vicinity. An appeal of this type suggests that there was every confidence of forming a permanent community as a place of worship is necessary, it also implied that these families had little collective wealth. The appeal did not fail, and with the support of the Chief Rabbi, the community decided to purchase and refit the old Art College in Paradise Lane, which was consecrated in September of that year. This was the first major event in the life of the community and attracted visitors from outside the town. With the establishment of the synagogue and the appointment of its first minister, Rev. I. Gallant, Jewry was placed on the map. Within a year the trustees were threatened with legal action over their inability to meet outstanding debts. This situation demonstrated the impoverishment of the community which had now grown to around fifty families and it was left to the Chief Rabbi, by an appeal, to save the synagogue from financial collapse.

Because of the fear of anti-semitism, the Jewish authorities at this time attempted to *"Anglicize"* the newly-arrived immigrants and endeavoured wherever possible to mould them into respectability and thus acceptance. In 1896 Blackburn was included in the Chief Rabbi's pastoral tour and the town received him in May. In the presence of the Lord Mayor and other civic dignatories he appealed to the community to donate to the Blackburn and East Lancs. Infirmary, an act that would gain it credibility and respectability.

It must be remembered however, that although the community was hardworking, poverty was never far away. At the turn of the century the majority of Jews lived close to the town centre on its western side in an area bounded by King St. and Bank Top in the south, Preston New Road to the north, Northgate to the east and Saunders Road to the west. This area is divided by Montague St. which became home to several families. Following the classic trades of the Jewish immigrant, by 1906 some fifteen Jewish tailors were established. They would work for the well established merchant tailors, take on private customers or eventually manage a combination of both. Their work took place in small workshops and

117

they would employ co-religionists, and of course family, in the enterprise, often going to Manchester to recruit labour. If tailoring was a main occupation, market trading and general dealing came a close second. Market Standers would sell cheap jewelry, fancy goods, optical goods, sponges, boots and shoes, leathers and textile piece goods. In addition there were a small number of cabinet makers, glaziers, (important in mill towns), picture framers and shopkeepers. These were the traditional trades and few Jews if any joined the ranks of the classic proletariat as factory or mill workers. Furthermore, no member of the community at this period had entered the liberal professions, this would be the experience of future generations. However, opting to live outside of large Jewish communities demonstrated a strong will to succeed. Indeed, the son of a prominent picture-framing family (the Rozensons), founded the Great Universal Stores whilst the son of a synagogue minister became a world renowned economist, (Eli Devons).

Apart from establishing a synagogue another crucial necessity for a Jewish community is a burial ground. As early as 1896 a plot was requested but refused by the local authority, a refusal that brought criticism from the *Blackburn Weekly Standard and Express* which detected an element of anti-semitism in the decision. However two years later a plot was set aside in the municipal cemetery and this important element for the community was secured.

If the first visit of the Chief Rabbi was an unqualified success his second, in 1899, took place under different circumstances. This was a result of an incident which highlighted the turbulent character of an unsophisticated, fractious Jewish community. In a small community like Blackburn where the immigrants were striving to raise themselves, often in a harsh world, status inside the community often revolved around positions within the synagogue. What started as an argument between a retiring member of the synagogue executive and other members at the 1899 annual general meeting ended up in a bout of fisticuffs principally involving two families. Summonses were issued and the Chief Rabbi had to intervene to help keep the incident out of the press and courts. Whilst the affair was settled, a breakaway synagogue was founded but did not last long. However, by 1904 another synagogue was formed to last three years. These events simply demonstrated how members of the community brought with them a predisposition to argue and dispute, a characteristic of Jewish life now part and parcel of its own folk-lore.

By 1914 the community had reached its height. It had established its main religious, social and cultural institutions and agencies and was probably the third largest Jewish community in Lancashire.

Because of the occupational structure of the community and its size the Jews of Blackburn did not have a high visibility. It was well integrated, its Working Men's Club open to non-Jews and its members contributing to non-Jewish causes. Inevitably, the fortunes of this type of community reflected the fortunes of the town in general. The inter-war decline of Blackburn led to the decline of the community. This, coupled with the inability of a small community to maintain its numbers as younger members left on marriage or to join larger communities like Manchester or Liverpool.

The community was augmented in the thirties by refugees escaping from Nazi Germany. Some of them were directed to stricken areas like Blackburn because of their entrepreunerial skills, but this was to be the last influx. It is not without a sense of sadness that the small cemetery remains the only obvious testament to the presence of this once boisterous community.

Congregationalism in Blackburn

Rev. Chris Damp

Congregationalism is a system of church order where each church is independent, and is governed by its own members. Blackburn had, like most towns, a number of Congregational churches. W.A. Abram listed ten Congregational churches in his book 'A Century of Independency in Blackburn' (1878).

The first Congregational church in Blackburn was founded in 1777 by Rev. James McQuhae, minister of the Congregational church meeting in the old chapel at Tockholes. He was a Scot and many of the Scots living in Blackburn travelled to Tockholes for worship. These people persuaded Mr. McQuhae to move to Blackburn and found a Congregational church in the town. It is unusual that a town the size of Blackburn had no Congregational church prior to this time, but this was perhaps due to there being a good number of Congregational churches in the district to which nonconformists living in Blackburn could travel. These included Wymondhouses, a church meeting at Hoghton Tower, Lower Chapel, Darwen and of course Tockholes.

A chapel was built immediately in a field called the Bull-meadow and was completed before May 1778. As the town grew houses were built about the chapel and the road on which the chapel stood became known as Chapel Street. The foundation stone of a new chapel was laid in April 1873 and was described as *"one of the noblest looking in the country"*. Sadly this fine building is now demolished, but the spire still stands, marking the site of Blackburn's first Congregational chapel.

Other Congregational churches in the town were founded at James Street 1841; Mill Hill 1847; Furthergate 1852; Nova Scotia 1855; Ramsgrave 1855; Park Road 1857; Bank Top 1860; Montague Street 1864; Audley Range 1878; Whitton 1884; Four Lane Ends 1885; Cherry Tree 1888; Feniscowles 1898; Brownhill 1928.

By 1972 only the churches at Chapel Street, Brownhill, Audley Range, Cherry Tree, Four Lane Ends, Furthergate, Mill Hill and Whitton survived. All of these churches united with the

Presbyterian Church of England and became members of the newly formed United Reformed Church, bringing about the end of Congregationalism in Blackburn itself.

Blackburn became a strong centre of Congregationalism and many famous ministers served some of the Blackburn churches. One of these ministers, Rev. Joseph Fletcher of Chapel Street, became the first tutor of the Blackburn Independent Academy whose object was *"to educate young men of decided Christian piety and competent talents for the Christian ministry, combining, as much as possible, with the permanent supply of the churches, the furtherance of the gospel, by itinerating labours, in this and neighbouring counties".* This was founded in 1816 by the Lancashire Congregational Union and the first student was admitted in the September. In 1823, Dr. Fletcher removed to London and was succeeded by Rev. Dr. George Payne. At its height the academy had twenty students in training at one time. In 1839, the committee of the academy met to discuss its future. It was felt that to further the work of the academy, the institution should move to Manchester. The buildings in Blackburn were too small and provided limited facilities. It was therefore resolved to erect a new college building in Manchester and this was opened in April 1843, the students, remaining at Blackburn, moving to the new buildings in Manchester. The college continued in Manchester until the early 1980s when the buildings were closed and the college united with the Methodist and Baptist colleges in Manchester.

Blackburn was for many years a centre of Congregationalism. Further reading on Blackburn Congregationalism can be found in Abram's book *Independency in Blackburn* (Blackburn 1878); B. Nightingale *Lancashire Nonconformity* vol. 2 (Manchester 1891), and in Richard Slate's *Rise and Progress of the Lancashire Congregational Union*, (London, 1840) there is a chapter about the Blackburn Independent Academy.

*   *   *   *   *

In 1836, Blackburn Academy threw out a student because he had *"fallen into levities and been guilty of indiscretion."*

This extracted from an *Annual Report of the Committee of Blackburn Independent Academy for the Education of Pious Young Men for the Christian Ministry.*

*   *   *   *   *

Four Square to the Wind on the Lofty Heights of Livesey — New Row Methodist Chapel

Alan D. Pickering

Writing about New Row Methodist Chapel in his *"History of Blackburn"* (1977) Abram said, " ..... *a Methodist Society was founded in Lower Darwen by Wesley himself, who preached in the village in 1759 and in 1761. An early preaching place of this Society was a farmhouse at T' Top o' th' Coal-Pits; and another was at New Row, a hamlet on the borders of Lower Darwen and Livesey, by the road from Blackburn to Tockholes. At New Row a Chapel was built in 1828 which is yet in use, and was rendered more commodious by the addition of galleries about twenty years ago. The chapel is served from Blackburn and contains about 400 sittings."*

Whittle, in his book *"Blackburn As It Is"* (1852), mentions the chapel briefly, and states in the description of the Townshnip of Livesey *"The Wesleyans have a chapel dated 1828. There is a school."*

We know that Wesley visited the area in 1785. He wrote in his diary:-

April 16   I had designed to go from Wigan to Blackburn, but hearing that one of our Society from Preston was at the point of death, I turned a little out of my way to spend half an hour with her. In the evening I preached at Blackburn, where the Society also is lively and continuing.

April 18   After preaching to a numerous congregation (but no one rich or well-dressed person among them, either morning or evening. Poor Blackburn!) I hastened to Gisburn.

April 21   I went through miserable roads to Blackburn, where notwithstanding the continuous rain, the new preaching house was filled with serious well-behaved people.

The datestone above the front door has the inscription G W T 1828 the GWT being Mr G.W. Turner who was a calico printer with a business in Stakes Hall, Mill Hill, without whose gift of the land for the Chapel and Burial ground, New Row might never have been chosen as the site for the Chapel, for one proposal was to build lower down Hey's Lane.

The first recorded burial at New Row Chapel was in 1850 when James Haworth of New Row was laid to rest, aged five months seventeen days.

The burial service was performed by Benjamin Clayton, and was the only burial to take place for the next two years.

The address of the deceased in many of the early burials at New Row is given as just *"New Row"*. This at first glance indicates that the deceased was from the area around the chapel which came to be known as New Row, but other addresses in the ledger give a much more specific address. It is my belief that *"New Row"* was *"Farmers Row"*. Evidence of this can be found in the ledger in the following entries.

William Lucas   *6 New Road, Livesey, Blackburn.*
Buried 25th June 1892.
Aged. 74 Years

Alice Lucas   *6 Farmers Row. New Row.*
Buried 9th October 1895.
Aged. 72 Years

An indication of how hard times were for the working class and underprivileged members of society can be seen in the chapel's early burial records. A high percentage of burials are of babies, infants and young people. Diet, poor living conditions, cold and damp, and ignorance of healthy living caused by poverty were the causes. This often resulted in families losing many members to illnesses which we today can avoid with ease.

A sad example of this can be seen in the entries showing Gertrude Holgate and Amy Holgate of Longhsaw Farm and both buried December 14th 1885. They were twin sisters, aged thirteen months.

An original record of the cost of a burial still survives. It is hand written on a paper adhered to the inside cover the first register and goes as follows:-

Funeral Dues of the Wesleyan Chapel New Row

Members and seat Holders	Not members nor seat Holders
One day to five years old	One day to five years old
s d	s d
7 6	9 0
From five to ten	From five to ten
s d	s d
9 0	12 0
From ten to fifteen	From ten to fifteen
s d	s d
12 0	15 0
From fifteen upwards	Fifteen upwards
s d	s d
15 0	18 0

The Seat Holders who paid a subscription for use of certain box pews in the Gallery had some privileges, which the example on the previous page shows. They were usually families who worshipped regularly together.

Almost all the original box pews still survive. The back row had to be removed recently for major repair to one of the beams supporting the Gallery.

A few of the old offertory collection boxes, with long handles to enable the collector to reach the occupants of the pews without entering them, still survive.

The year 1905 brought the centenary of the New Row Methodist Society, and to commemorate this event two stained glass windows were placed in the north wall of the Chapel.

The window on the left looking from inside carries the following inscription:-

To the glory of God in memory of Robert Worswick formerly superintendant of this Sunday School died 28th April 1901. Also of Mary Ann his devoted wife died July 13th 1903. Say ye to the righteous it shall be well with them.

The window to the right, which was taken out and restored in 1986, carries the following inscription:-

This window was placed to commemorate the Centenary of the Chapel and Sunday School and to the honour of all the past and present workers 1805 - 1905. Sabbath Schools are England's glory.

The Pulpit, Organ and Choir Stalls were all put in the Chapel at the same time in the year 1878, at a total cost of £200. A small brass plaque can be seen on the Organ with the inscription:-

"Alexander Young & Son, Builders, Manchester. 1878"

The Organ, although still complete and in working order, requires a complete overhaul and is no longer used.

* * *

Here is a list of the Trustees of New Row Chapel in the year 1860. (The original deed is lost and the Trustees' names not known). James Foulds - New Row; Robert Lacey - New Row; Thomas Lacey - New Row; John Cowell - New Row; John Neville - New Row; John Greaves - Blackburn; William Livesey - Blackburn; Thomas Charnley - Blackburn; J.S. Barton - Blackburn; John Thompson, draper, - Blackburn; Robert Bannister - Blackburn; Edward Gregson, Manufacturer - Blackburn; William Kaye- Darwen; Edward Gregson, druggist - Darwen; Thomas Holding - Darwen; Henry Ainsworth - Darwen.

Memories of the Blackburn Ragged School

Rev. Walter Fancutt

I was born at 36 Lawrence Street, Blackburn, on the 22nd February, 1911 and was taken to the Ragged School very early in my life. The school had been founded in the year 1881 by J.T. Walkden and James Dixon, in a small building at the corner of Lune Street and Leyland Street. This building was demolished in 1895 and the fine buildings in Bent Street were erected, to be opened by Earl Compton on July 3rd, 1897. Besides the School, the Trustees also opened a house in Fielden Street as a Girls' Rest, and another in Paradise Terrace as a Boys' Home. Later, these led to the Blackburn Orphanage, a building costing about £6,000.

The work of the Ragged School was so successful that, in 1908, an extension was built in Bent Street, we always called it *"the new wing"*. Besides a ground floor hall seating about 200 people where we held Christian Endeavour Meetings and Sunday Bible Classes for men, there were five class rooms. In my own day, 1917-31, I well remember the wonderful Sundays when twelve class rooms and three large halls were well filled with about 400 children and many adults.

Mr. Jesse Chilman was the General Superintendent in my day. Richard Haworth took the men's class, and Anthony Billington led the large children's school. Nancy Ellen was leader of the Primary Department which met in a hall off the ground floor schoolrooms. Her department had a series of tiered benches on which the children sat, and on the front wall there was a painting of a great eye, about four feet across, beneath which was the text, *"Thou God seest me"*. *(Gen. 16.13)*. I imagine the text was supposed to give the little ones comfort but for many of us, in our childhood, it was a reminder that, if we did wrong, that eternal eye would see us! When we moved up from Primary to Junior, and from Junior to the *"upper School"*, it was always a great occasion and year by year we were given prizes for attendance.

In 1929 I went to Bible College in London. As there were no students grants in those days I would have had great difficulty

125

with out-of-pocket expenses had I not received a gift each month from the Ragged School! After the ordinary offering on a Sunday afternoon a small velvet bag, aptly called, *"Walter's bag"*, was passed round and each teacher made a small contribution! For two years, that bag produced most of what I needed, apart from college fees which were seen to by the Ragged School Trustees and St. Michael's Church, Blackburn.

From 1903 A Lad's Club was opened at the Ragged School each Monday and Friday. About 300 members were registered in my years. For the girls, Richard Haworth, an Art Dealer, arranged for drill, dressmaking, first-aid, elocution etc., to be available and about a hundred girls were on the register most years. The boys had a similar organisation, the *"Boy Naturalists"*, who marched through, and out of the town with their Bugle Band, to spend the afternoon each Saturday in the country. This group, founded in 1910 was a great joy to us and we were proud of our uniform, which consisted of a white shirt, blue tie, red sash and brown haversack.

Each Sunday, worship in the Upper School was led by an orchestra of 24 players, conducted and trained by Clarence Isherwood, a local weaver who was a magnificent musician.

Every year, we looked forward to many special events including field days, canal boat trips and, best of all, an annual trip to St. Annes on Sea under *"Pearson's Fresh Air Fund"*. On that day, two special trains left Blackburn for the sand and sea. For many of us, it was the one visit to the seaside for a whole year. As we marched from the station to the sandy dunes, lorries would pass, filled with delicious food, Tattersall's pies, cakes and barrels of tea and coffee, which were served to us as we sat in circles by the sea.

I never knew Mr. Walkden, but his fellow-founder, James Dixon, lived on until 1936 and during my days at the School, we were always pleased to see the venerable gentleman as he visited the School from time to time.

I still look forward to receiving the monthly magazine of the Ragged School which is sent to me by the present superintendent, Alan R. Barnes, who continues the great tradition of Christian fellowship and service at the School. The main building is now a Day Centre which caters for Blackburnians in special need, whilst the New Wing - as we called it - offers the same facilities of worship and leisure activities of those which made the School such a blessing to us. Long may it continue.

The Treacle Mines at Tockholes

Nick Howorth

When I was a lad in Blackburn we used to live at Queen's Park. In the 1940s, during the war, there wasn't much outdoors entertainment apart from occasional visits to Ewood Park where we watched the Rovers from stacks of wooden boxes for use at the nearby *'fuse factory'* at the top of Stopes Brow. At weekends we used to play in streams and in disused quarries, but we also liked walking over the local fields and moors. One of my best pals had a Gran who lived about 4 miles away in a small cottage near the parish church of St Stephen, down the steep hill by the Rock Inn at Tockholes (pronounced 'Tockles' by the locals). The old lady drew her drinking water from a spring in the garden wall across the road, and the cottage had an earth privy in the back garden. It has been gentrified (tarted-up) since then. Sometimes on a hot summer's day the two of us would walk over to see his Gran. It was a hilly walk; up past Queen's Park Hospital, down to lower Darwen. Then past the Golden Cup (t'Gowd Cup) up Bog Height Road, and over the fields to Tockholes. We arrived a big powfagged. A cup of spring water and a barm cake worked wonders.

The story told about Tockholes both then and now was that there used to be treacle mines there dating back to the Roman occupation. I still have a faded newspaper cutting from the Northern Daily Telegraph showing Julius Caesar's thumbprint found in the mines at Tockholes. I thought the truth was probably that black muddy water sometimes seeped out of the side of some hills on the moors from abandoned mines up there. Some of the old shafts are still fenced off to protect the sheep grazing the moors.

Not much happened on the treacle mines story over the next 40 years. I used to walk, and still do, from time to time over Darwen and Turton moors, using the Black Dog at Belmont as a base. It is still a proper gradely little pub, and there's not many left, I can tell you. Then, one day in 1987, I came across a short article by Dr J.T. Hughes of Oxford called *'The truth about treacle'* in which he explained the true origins of the treacle well described in chapter 7 of Lewis Carroll's book *'Alice in Wonderland'*. Chapter 7 entitled *'A mad tea-party'* tells of three sisters who lived on treacle at the bottom of a well. All Lewis Carroll's stories were based on real people, places and events. This story was based upon the holy well at Binsey, near Oxford, associated with St Frideswide, and famous for its miraculous cures. The word *'treacle'* is derived from an old word meaning a medicinal remedy (Middle English *tryacle,* or *triacle,* from the Latin *triaca,* or *theriaca*). The penny dropped at once - Tockholes had **two** claims to fame: its treacle mines **and** a holy well! I hadn't realised before that they were one and the same. The well is situated in the grounds of the ruined Hollinshead Hall at Tockholes. No-one knows how long it has been there, but ancient records show that Hollinshead first belonged to the Radcliffes of Ordsall in the reign of Edward II. Today the well is preserved in an old Well House restored early this century by Liverpool Corporation who owned the nearby reservoirs and waterworks. So it seemed clear to me that somehow, over the years, the existence of the holy well, or treacle well, at Hollinshead had become a *'humorous'* story about treacle mines.

It is curious that a similar fate has overtaken the wells at the Nick of Pendle near the Wellsprings Hotel. There is a story about treacle mines there, with the treacle being used to make flypaper for over 200 years. An old Blackburnian once told me that Mile End Row, off Revidge Road, on the west side of the town, used to be called *'Treacle Row'* when he was a boy, although he did not understand the significance of the name. At the far end of Mile End Row there used to be a field (now garages) behind St Silas's Church, which, in my youth contained the ruins of an old well house. Mile End Row and the parallel West View Place (formerly *'Double Street'*) are some of the oldest remaining parts of Blackburn. The two streets were a hand-loom weavers' community, as can be seen from the architecture of the surviving cottages. The remains of an old fortified farmhouse damaged in the Civil War are preserved as a listed building behind the West View Hotel. This was probably the famous Christmas Eve skirmish of 1642 when Sir Gilbert Hoghton's Royalists invaded Blackburn from Mellor via Revidge and down Duke's Brow.

Allen Clarke has a section on a holy well on Halliwell moors near Bolton in his book *'Moorlands and Memories'* published in 1924. He tells of the old Lancashire custom of well dressing on May Day, the first day of summer in the old church calendar. Young boys and girls used to walk out to holy wells on May Day; the girls would lay wild flowers and drink some water to improve their looks. My mother told me that well dressing is still done in some Derbyshire villages. Presumably the industrial revolution led to the demise of May Day ceremonies in Lancashire, and as collective public memory about the true significance of treacle wells was forgotten, so, nonsense stories akin to children's folklore have gained currency to account for treacle mines.

Blackburn's Licensed Houses in the Late 19th Century

In 1892, the Blackburn Magistrates took steps to survey the whole of the licensed houses in the borough. They divided the town into five districts and divided themselves into five groups to examine all the 254 fully-licensed houses, the 206 beer-houses (where beer could be sold) and the 35 off-licensed houses, where only beer could be sold for consumption off the premises.

Each group was accompanied by the Chief Constable, Mr. Lewis, and the Magistrates' Clerk, Mr. Brothers, on their inspections, which took place in April and May 1893.

They reported together in July. Their report makes fascinating reading, as well as being informative of social conditions.

Their first conclusion was that certain areas of town - principally the older ones - were *"congested"* wth licensed premises. their report listed each premise and told, amongst other things, how far each one was away from its nearest neighbour. *"The Farmer's Boy"*, 93 Heys Lane, was 900 yards away from the next licensed house - and this was the greatest distance between any. Most were less than 100 yards apart. Clearly, Mrs Bayly, a Temperance worker reporting on her visit to Blackburn 30 years before was correct in her observation that drink was the cause of many of Blackburn's social problems, including much poverty. The town's M.P. John Morley spoke two years previous to the report in Manchester's Free Trade Hall on the issue and renewal of licences for the sale of intoxicating liquor. For too long, the magistrates had failed to heed voices raised which were concerned over the number of licensed houses and the power of the brewers.

The magistrates called upon the Licensing Justices, who are certain magistrates sitting as a separate body, to consider the state of affairs they reported upon, and, by implication, reduce the numbers. They recalled that the greatest number of drunkenness cases arose in *"the congested areas"*.

Speaking of the quality and suitability of the buildings, they found that, of the fully-licensed houses, 11 were first class, 119 good, 92 fair and 32 poor. Of the beer-houses, 2 were first class, 12 good, 101 fair and 91 were poor. Clearly, some of the breweries had been spending money on new buildings, but still kept on those at the lower end of the quality line. Mrs Bayly had commented on this too.

The adequacy of the buildings' design so far as to allow for good police supervision was another matter highlighted in the report. Many houses had back yards shared with others. 59 fully-licensed houses and 109 beer-houses failed to meet with approval in this respect, and *"should be remedied immediately"*. The desired standard should be that each house should have its own back yard, which should not have a back entrance. If this were achieved, *"it would, to a good extent, put an end to illicit Sunday drinking, which the police have every reason to believe is extensively carried on in our midst ..."*

The report criticised the system of the tenanting of houses by the breweries. It lead to dirty premises. Some of the rooms inspected *"had not been touched with paper or paint for over thirty years."*

97 of the fully-licensed houses had no stables attached, and 52 had stables which were let off to others.

No beds were provided for travellers in 153 fully-licensed houses, nor did they provide refreshments other than drink.

Only 43 of the 495 were *"free houses"*, a proportion of eleven to one in favour of *"tied houses"* which the justices considered an objectionable system. It forced tenants to sell drink by illegitimate means.

Clearly, the magistrates felt that many of the beer-houses should be got rid of, although, because they had all been licensed before 1869, the refusal of their licences could only be made on the four grounds named in the Act of that year.

It came as a surprise to the justices to learn that only 39 houses had bathroom accommodation.

Many of the licensees spoken to agreed that there were far too many licensed houses in the town, both for good government and trade. One of the beer-houses visited was closed for business as well as inspection - it was only 25 yards from another beer-house, 42 yards from a fully licensed house *"and has had seven different tenants within the last three years"*.

The report had some effect. At the next Brewster (Licensing) Sessions, 24 licensees lost their licences.

Blackburn's First Brewery (?)

Ian Sutton

That Blackburn has a long pedigree of brewing is well known, and there are several names mentioned when discussion arises as to which was the first commercial brewery in this beery town. Dutton's?, Thwaite's?, Nuttall's?, Matthew Brown's? The answer is - none of these. Accepting that small breweries attached to beerhouses be ignored, it is almost certain that the answer is *"Park Place Brewery"*.

An early clue to the existence of a brewery in the town before this date can be traced in Dr. Aikin's famous topographical book: *"A description of the county from 30 to 40 miles around Manchester"* which was published in 1795. If one examines the brief summary of the town the existence and possible location of the site is given:

"To the east of Blackburn is fore-gate, where are some good new buildings. The new road to Haslingden, Bury and Manchester passes this way. A little to the south is a capital brewery, close by which the new canal from Leeds to Liverpool takes its course."

Judging from this description Dr. Aikin took time off from his travels to sample the local brew, which obviously met his satisfaction! Through this description the brewery can probably be identified on the earliest accurate map of the town produced in 1822, which shows some industrial buildings at Park Place, close by a bridge over the canal.

So the brewery certainly seems to have been in production in 1795 - one needs to go back further to trace its origins.

The brewery was probably erected during 1793 by John Nicholls who formed a partnership with other local businessmen and shop owners and began to trade under the name Nicholls and Co. The full partnership consisted of: John Nicholls, Peter Ellingthorp, Richard Meanley, William Hewitt and William Stackhouse. The brewery itself was opened or began production on 5th February 1794 and judging by a report in the local paper was certainly popular with the editor who spoke of it as *"rendering an essential service to the middling and lower class of the people"* and went on to wish that the proprietors *"heartily meet with public encouragement and be crowned with success".*

It seems that Mr. Nicholls and the partnership had put a great deal of money into the venture. No expense was spared, and the brewery was described as being *"second to none in the county"*. They certainly didn't start up in a half-hearted manner and were obviously expecting to make a large success of the venture as they had bought large supplies of *"every material used in the making of ale from the best markets"* and employed *"the most judicious brewers and workmen that could be acquired"*. Judging from this last statement neither John Nicholls nor any of the partners were experienced brewers themselves, they merely injected capital into a venture hoping that it would come off, either that or they saw a sizeable market for *"ale of different qualities to fruit every degree of purchaser"*.

The brewery seems to have opened with a flourish, a report in the local paper a month after opening states:

"The new brewery in this town begins to show forth some of its salutory effects already - in the houses of the humble industrious handicraftmen, as well as the cellars of the more opulent, a sound, wholesome and exhilarting beverage is now to be met with, congenial not only to the palate but also to the pocket of the consumer".

Presumably Nicholls produced a variety of a good quality at a reasonable price and aimed them primarily not at public houses or beerhouses but at individuals for home consumption. One must not forget that, at this time, the vast majority of public houses had their own brewhouse attached and brewed their own distinct ales.

Within a short time the brewery had achieved a reputation for either producing fine ales or at least some product which differed from other local brews as they began to attract customers from neighbouring areas. A typically patriotic newspaper report in April of that year illustrates this point in an amusing story:

"A few particular and truly loyal sons of Britain, in the county, hearing of the fame and excellence of the ale lately manufactured at the new brewery, at Park Place, near this town, determined on regaling themselves therewithin; and having procured an invitation from a friend in town, whose cellar was well stored with that salubrious elevator of the spirits, they accordingly met in a select manner, at his house, on Thursday evening last, when, after having in the most profuse manner spent their opinions in favour of the liquor, the glass pushed merrily round, which naturally produced a number of loyal and patriotic songs, toasts and sentiments among which were the following, commencing with the never to be forgotten loyal toast by Britons of: The King, Queen and the Royal family - the Prince of Wales - the Duke of York, and the British Army - The British Navy and our persevering Admirals and

invincible tars - the encouragement of Agriculture in this Kingdom - the town of Blackburn and cotton manufacture - the new brewery and the generous manufacturers who study the public interest as well as their own. The evening having concluded as it passed, in the most cordial friendship and conviviality, the company returned, well pleased with the adventure to their respective places of abode ".

It would seem that the brewery had got off to a good start and was trading quite briskly at this period, however by the end of the year things were not progressing so smoothly. In July, the existing partnership came to a close:

"The partnership between us, the undersigned, John Nicholls, Peter Ellingthorp, Richard Meanley, William Hewitt and William Stackhouse, carrying on business as common brewers at Blackburn aforesaid, under the firm of Nicholls and Co. was this day dissolved by mutual consent .... All debts due to, and owing by the said partnership will be received and paid by the said Peter Ellingthorp, Richard Meanley, William Hewitt and William Stackhouse - as witness our hands."

In other words for some reason John Nicholls left the partnership and the brewery began to trade under the name of Richard Meanley and Co. Whether John Nicholls died, retired or just purely left the company is not known and the company seems to have carried on without addition to the existing partnership with Richard Meanley taking the helm.

The brewery was still on firm footing and by winter that year placed an advert in the local paper:

"To the public:-

Blackburn 10th December 1794

The brewery being situated out of town, and from the shortness of the days at this season of the year, it may be inconvenient for the people who live at some distance, as well as others in the Town, to walk so far; Therefore a book will be constantly kept at Mr. Stackhouse's shop, to take down the orders of those who may be in want of Ale or Beer, which will be duly attended to, and all favours gratefully acknowledged."

The brewery itself was situated about half a mile outside the town alongside the Leeds - Liverpool canal (which was still in a state of construction at this time). Although the area boasted a few houses and mills there was very little built between Park Place and the town itself, indeed they were separated by the Town's Moor although the coaching route from Haslingden to Blackburn bisected the moor and connected the town to Park Place. It seemd a strange decision to build the brewery in this location instead of within the town although the building of the canal would undoubtedly have influenced John Nicholls because of the transport benefits. There was also a good supply of pure water in this area from natural springs and brooks whereas picking a suitable site within the town could have proved more difficult.

The company continued satisfactorily for the next four years when Peter Ellingthorp withdrew from the partnership. The reasons for this are unknown. He was to continue in his profession as an attorney until he died in 1807. The three remaining partners carried on, asking for: "... *all persons who stand indebted to the old partnership concern are requested to pay their debts immediately to the said Mr. Meanley, otherwise legal measures will be taken for recovery thereof.*"

Perhaps this is an indication that all was not well. Competition had become fierce. As well as the brewery set up by Thomas Dutton in 1799 in the centre of Blackburn, there were said to be around 92 public houses (excluding Beerhouses) brewing their own beer and ales - a large number for such a town. Reformers of the late 1700's were concerned with the drinking habits, morals and manners of working class towns such as Blackburn and there was a general tightening up of the issue and renewal of licences for the sale of beer. The Brewster sessions invited complaints from people of any misconduct committed by any licence holder, and transfer of licences required the consent of Justices for the first time. The "*Sale of Beer Act*" (1795) was a vast step forward in the growing battle over control of licenced premises and drunkenness.

The company survived in this format until the following year when Richard Meanley withdrew himself from the concern stating that all debts owing to and from the concern would be received and paid by himself. Meanley seems to have been the mainstay of the company and without his financial backing Hewitt and Stackhouse could not afford to run the company between them. They looked for, and found, two new partners, namely James Wood and John Walch and from 17th May 1803 began to trade under the name of Wood, Hewitt and Co.

In 1807 two quarter shares in the brewery were put up for sale possibly belonging to James Wood and John Walch, applications were to be sent to either James Wood on the premises or Mr. Hewitt, Clare St., Liverpool; Mr. Hewitt, Ardwick, Manchester or Mr. P. Hewitt, Bolton. One presumes that Hewitt was not involved solely in the brewing trade but was a businessman and partner in various ventures. The description of the brewery states it to extend upwards of 100 yards along the line of the canal. The water flowed into the brewery "*from such a level as to render pumps unnecessary*" and is described as "*abundant*". The water was

134

conveyed to the vats through pipes leading from the boiler and also turned a water wheel eleven yards in diameter which was used for grinding the malt. The buildings consisted of *"a good dwelling house, the brewery, stables, cart sheds"*. All the utensils were in excellent condition *"commodiously arranged for the brewing of Porter, Ale and table beer."* It was also stated that the brewery could be extended, suggesting that it was not hemmed in amongst the other houses and mills in the area.

Whether anyone took up the offer to buy the quarter shares is not known, but the brewery itself was put up for sale in 1809 without any mention of Messrs' Wood and Walch being still involved, indicating that they probably did leave the concern in 1807. With only Stackhouse and Hewitt involved the brewery was again short of capital and an attempt to raise some in 1811 resulted in part of the brewery buildings being sold to Messrs. Edward Walsh and Co.

Futher crises then hit the brewery, William Stackhouse was declared bankrupt and Edward Walsh and Co. auctioned a quarter share in the brewery which included the buildings and yards etc. It is probable that this was the end of the brewery or at least the beginning of the end. No further details concerning its running or existence of the brewery can be traced until 1817 when the buildings, premises and equipment were sold by auction. The premises are described as being a *"former Public Ale and Porter Brewery - at present untenanted"*. A list of the items to be auctioned indicates its size:

"The premises consist of a large brewing house and store rooms, with numerous and convenient offices, a comfortable dwelling house, cottage, stable. They are capable of being converted at a moderate expense into a corn mill and corn warehouse, cotton factory, foundry, machine makers etc.

A plot of valuable land, 1750 sq. yards adjoining road and leading to above premises.

A variety of brewing fixtures, implements and utensils, comprising: 1 large water wheel, and cistern to ditto. 1 stage round mash tub. 1 large malt mill with rollers. 2 large copper pans, 29 cwt. 2 qrs. 8 lbs. 1 large copper pan, 15 cwt. 2 qrs. 9 lbs. Back over copper pan 8 cwt. Large mash tub. Cover for ditto. 1 hop back. 1 cooler. Step ladder to 1st cooler. Windlass. 2 large rounds. 2 large Porter vats containing 240 barrels.

Further applications regarding the sale were available from Pitt, Hewitt Esq. of Bolton. There was probably some connection between this firm and William Hewitt.

Whoever bought the premises didn't remain there long as it was again for sale in 1819, being advertised as *"3 storeys, 40 yards long, formerly a brewery."* The brewery premises appear to have ended up as a cotton mill owned by a J. Haughton, the J.P.'s report of 1823 on cotton mills in Blackburn showed the mill at Park Place to be very dirty and had not been whitewashed for a long time and employed a small workforce of about 40. The Factory Commission reports of 1833 showed that J. Haughton and Sons, Park Place had started the mill about 12 years previously, (i.e. c1821). This adds weight to the theory that they were using the old brewery buildings, or at least part of them. Presumably they didn't have the capital to erect their own mill, so took over the existing premises.

In 1837 an auction of Haughton's land in Park Place shows that the brewery site was relatively unaltered when compared with the 1822 map. However by the 1850's the mill had been enlarged and became part of the Park Place Cotton Mills.

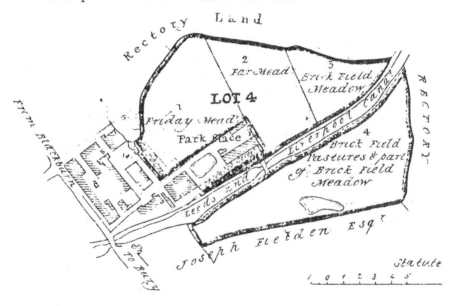

The life of the Park Place brewery was a relatively short one. Built in 1793, commencing brewing in 1794 and ceasing between 1811-1814. (In 1814 the only brewers listed in Blackburn are: George Blelock, Jubilee Brewery, Darwen St., Duckworth, Clayton and Thwaites, Eanam Brewery and Dutton and Son, Salford Brewery.) A sad end for Blackburn's first public brewery, However, it is at least remembered by the small bridge over the canal - *"Brewery Bridge".*

Blackburn and The Canal

Alan Duckworth

Time was when *"The Blackburn Mail"* featured a regular shipping list detailing the comings and goings of vessels named *Dispatch, Heart of Oak, Defiance,* and *Nelson,* and indeed it isn't hard to imagine the taproom crowds in the old, bow-windowed taverns of the *"Barbary Coast"* falling silent when an old salt began yarning of his adventures afloat.

The time was 1810 and the heroically-named vessels doing their bit in the ongoing struggle against Napoleon were barges. They carried puncheons of molasses, hogsheads of tallow and bales of yarn to and from the newly opened wharf at Eanam. The Leeds and Liverpool canal had come to Blackburn.

The Industrial Revolution was born in the 18th century, but its development was hindered by communication difficulties. The roads were bad and the Pennines formed a barrier between the fledgling cotton industry of Lancashire and the growing woollen industry of Yorkshire. In 1761 the Duke of Bridgewater had opened a canal from his coal mines at Worsley to Manchester. The success of this venture encouraged industrialists to look at other possibilities. The first public call for a canal to link the rivers Aire and Mersey seems to have been made in 1764. The Bridgewater canal had been engineered by James Brindley and it was Brindley who made the first survey of the Leeds and Liverpool canal. As might be expected, it took some time to reconcile the Yorkshire and Lancashire interests, but in 1770 the necessary Act of Parliament was obtained.

Work began near Blackburn in 1796, but it wasn't until 1810 that the canal joined Blackburn with Leeds. A procession of 27 vessels decorated with flags, some with bands on board, sailed into the town from Henfield, (Clayton-le-Moors). At every bridge enthusiastic members of the crowd attempted to board the passing vessels. It was estimated that as many as 25,000 people gathered at Eanam to celebrate the opening of the canal. Such a crowd had probably never been seen before in Blackburn and would not be seen again until the town's football team began its glory days towards the end of the century. The celebrations continued into the evening at the New Inn, the Castle, the Bay Horse and other hostelries in the town.

The last section of the canal, that between Blackburn and Chorley was completed in 1816. Industry benefitted enormously from the canal, which was ideal for transporting material in bulk such as coal and limestone. Mills sprang up along the line of the canal particularly at Nova Scotia and Eanam. Passenger traffic too flourished. By the 1820's there was a regular passenger service between Blackburn and Burnley. The boats were covered with seats and had windows. Extra passengers could be accommodated on the flat roof. At night the boats were illuminated. They were pulled by 2 horses, both ridden, and one of the riders had a bugle to alert intending passengers of the boat's arrival. George Head in his *'Home Tour of the Manufacturing Districts of the North of England'* which he undertook in 1835 describes being in such a boat: *"A rough set of people composed the company on boards ... All classes were jumbled together; groups of men and women dirtily dressed and noisy. The former smoked tobacco and guzzled beer; so also did the latter, besides occasionally picking periwinkles out of their shells with pins."*

The coming of the railways robbed the canals of their passenger traffic, though for the conveyance of goods in bulk they still had the advantage. The canals were nationalised in 1948 and in 1963 they came under the control of the British Waterways Board. Regular commercial traffic on the canal came to an end in 1972 when the delivery of coal to Wigan Power Station stopped. At 127 miles the Leeds and Liverpool canal is the longest in the country and in terms of amounts of goods carried it was probably the most successful. However, the end of commercial traffic is not the end of the story.

The leisure potential of the canal had been recognised early on by fishermen, by skaters on the canal's reservoir at Rishton and by boys and girls eager to bathe, particularly near Whitebirk Power Station where the water returned to the canal was warmer. Pleasure boating too soon became popular. In Summer, coal barges were cleaned out, seats were installed and excursions were made to resorts such as Whittle Springs, where the brewery was an added attraction.

In 1985 the canal corridor improvement scheme was set up by Lancashire County Council and Wigan Metropolitan Borough Council. The recent refurbishments at Eanam Wharf are a result of this venture. Clearly the canal is going to play as big a part in the town's developing tourism and heritage industry as it did nearly 200 years ago in the town's manufacturing industry.

Press Button "B" at Billinge End

In The National Telephone Journal of July 1907 appeared an article written by Mr C.J. Remington, the District Manager for the National Telephone Company. It was headed *"Kiosk Public Telephones"* and was written in response to one which had previously appeared on the subject of *"Street Call Offices"*. Mr Remington said that there were many telephone *"cabinets"* on railways stations, but considered these too small for use by persons often weighed down with umbrellas and parcels, in a hurry to catch a train. He hoped soon to see a cabinet of a larger size *"which would greatly conduce to the comfort of using the telephone from railway stations"*.

He went on to tell of a kiosk at a well-known Blackburn crossroads:-

"The accompanying illustrations show a kiosk of a somewhat picturesque type which was fitted up some time ago on the outskirts of Blackburn, and has proved an excellent revenue earner, besides being a good educator for the telephone service. As shown in one of the illustrations it is placed at a corner of four cross-roads (at the terminus of the Preston New Road tram section), and it is, therefore, in a most favourable position to catch the public eye. The idea of putting a call office at this place orginated with the late Mr. Eli Heyworth, but the estimated cost of the original design, some £80, was considered far too high, and the matter would have dropped had not Mr. Claxton suggested a **"rustic arbour"**, *such as are often used in gardens. This was bought for some £20; the thatched roof was replaced by wooden ribs to represent red tiles, and made thoroughly weather-proof. It is placed at the bottom corner on a piece of private ground abutting on the road, for which privilege the Company pay a small annual rent. The clock is the property of the Blackburn Corporation, and is placed there, by permission of the Company, for the use of the tramway officials for timing and regulating the tramway traffic at this terminus. The police have a key of the door and are allowed to speak free from the call office to the police station; in return for this facility, they keep an eye on the kiosk. The public enter by placing one penny in the automatic box on the door. The door closes automatically, and when inside the*

public pay for local calls at call office rates, the fees being placed in the usual automatic box attached to the instrument. The kiosk has lately been lighted electrically, the light being switched on by shooting a bolt on the door from the inside when the caller enters; arrangements are now being made for exhibiting advertisements, from which the Company will secure some additional revenue. The inside measurements of the kiosk are 6 feet 6 inches by 5 feet 8 inches, and the roof is 8 feet from the floor in the centre, so it will be seen that it is quite a roomy call office. When first brought into use the table and seats bought with the kiosk were left in, but on the first Sunday four men were discovered by the police inside smoking and playing cards; consequently the facilites for this amusement were withdrawn and the trouble ceased. Indeed, the police look after this kiosk so well that, though far out of the town, we have no trouble with it."

The Teleghost

Pauline M. Hutchinson

A theatre stood in Jubilee Street, Blackburn, for over seventy years, first opening as *"Trevanion's Amphitheatre"*, later becoming the *"Prince's"*. In 1906 it was rebuilt and called the *"New Prince's"* till 1928, when it was renamed *"The Grand"*. In December 1931, it was used as a cinema for a short while before closing.

In 1934 it was purchased by a family firm - Will Murray & Sons - and reopened as a theatre. Will Murray ran *"Casey's Court"* (a kind of touring Fred Karnos Circus) which featured people like Charlie Chaplin. When the comedian Norman Wisdom came to the Grand after the last war, Mr. Murray told him to change his act. Norman did so and started to sing at Mr. Murray's request. He has never looked back since.

The theatre thrived, hosting famous names such as George Formby, Max Wall, Tessie O'Shea, Charlie Kunz, Jimmy Wheeler, Ted Ray and Norman Evans. In the 1950's, with the advent of television, the audiences dwindled - only 28 people on one occasion. In June, 1954, the Post Office expressed their interest in buying the building to build a five storey automatic telephone exchange to replace the manual exchanges in Darwen Street and Blakewater.

The theatre struggled on for another two years before finally closing it's doors on 21st January, 1956. The final show was a variety show by Blackburn artists entitled *'Blackburn Takes a (Final) Bow'*. Mr. Harry Rothwell, the ventriloquist in the final show, gave the first reports of ghostly happenings in the theatre. Lights used to come on by themselves and curtains which had been closed on the stage, would be found open. There would also be strange tapping noises on the pipes and from the dressing rooms.

The theatre stood idle for thirty months, during which time there were two fires under the stage, probably started by vagrants. The building was finally demolished in August, 1958. Blackburn Automatic Telephone Exchange was built on the site and opened officially in 1964.

The switchboard was manned through the night by three male

142

operators who have many tales to tell of unusual happenings which occurred in the early hours.

On one occasion, my husband Geoff, was on duty with George Grier and Bert Cottam. George had gone for his official break, leaving Geoff and Bert on the switchboard. It was past one o'clock and the number of calls coming through was slackening off, when they heard heavy footsteps thumping across the floor above. At first, it was assumed that it was George taking a bit of exercise, as he always wore heavy brogue shoes with steel heel tips. However, the night staff kitchen window was visible from the switchboard where the pair were sitting and on glancing up, they could see George standing at the kitchen window. The footsteps continued!

When George returned to the switchroom, he was a bit uneasy as Geoff and Bert related the happenings. After this incident, whenever George worked a through-night, he never ventured into the lounge or canteen on the floor above.

Another night operator, Joe Penketh, has also experienced strange happenings in the early hours. Joe has called the lift from the third floor, but it has not responded and so he had to walk down the stairs. Another time, he entered the lift on the third floor and pressed the button for the ground floor. After what seemed an eternity, when the doors opened again, he was still on the third floor!

At Christmas, a large tree was always provided in the switchroom, decorated with fairy lights and glass baubles. Early one Christmas morning, Ray Jackson heard rustling coming from the corner of the room occupied by the tree. He went to investigate twice, but could not find a reason for the noise. A few minutes after returning to his seat at the switchboard the second time, all the baubles fell off the tree onto the hard tiled floor. Not one was broken. This 'happening' was witnessed by the other operators on duty that night.

Many times, when all three telephonists were working at the switchboard, they heard the lift move up and down. Nobody else would be in the building and the front door would be locked! On other occasions, the venetian blinds have been known to rattle and waft out into the room, when there was not a breath of wind outside. A piano has been heard tinkling when there is no piano in the exchange! These events were always put down to 'Old Murray'.

In 1976, the Equal Rights Act was passed, allowing women to work through-nights. The men did their best to disuade the female staff from joining them, by telling tales of the Exchange ghost.

However, I was not to be deterred and was one of the first lady part time telephonists to change to full time and so work through the night.

I must admit that I have heard the lift move on its own but it has never bothered me. I have put it down to the powers of electronics rather than a ghost.

All the male operators who worked at the Exchange in the early days, have now either died or retired. Maybe the teleghost has also *'died'*.

144

Blackburn's Literary Associations

When considering the town's literary associations as a whole, it is probably true to say that Blackburn's reputation rests on its poets rather than its writers of prose. However, as there are several excellent Blackburn novelists writing now, that situation could well alter in future years. Today's writers are seldom held in the same regard as those who have passed on.

Although the town was visited and written about by pre-Victorian literary figures, the story really starts in Victoria's reign. The output of the mills and foundries can be equated to the output of writers in those times. The local journalist and poet John Walker (born 1845 in the town) said in 1891, *"Blackburn, it is safe to say, has produced more weavers of calico and of verse than any other town in the United Kingdom .... Within a mile from its busy centre, the workman can gain heights from which he may catch glimpses which will make him less forlorn ...."*Self-educated, a man of whom the town can be proud, he wrote in standard English and dialect. He wrote one of my favourite poems, *"Mi Grandad"*, the first verse of which is:-

Aw allus wur fond o' mi grandad,
  'Cause aw know he'd a likin' for me;
He're a rare owd chap, an' as kindly
  As ever a body could be.
Aw th' childer i' th'fowd gather'd reawnd him,
  When they see him come whooam fro' up t' street;
For they knew ther wur apples an' toffy,
  Or summat as nice an' as sweet.

That Blackburn produced more poets than any other town is, in my opinion, true. No other town can boast a book such as George Hull's *"The Poets and Poetry of Blackburn"*. Published in 1902, it is an essential item for anyone with Blackburn in their blood. George (born 1863 at Eanam) was a fine poet himself, and published books of his work.

Pre-eminent amongst Blackburn's poets when they regularly met in the town centre public house aptly named *"The Poet's Corner"* was William Billington (born 1827 at Salmesbury, died 1884). After a life-time of rhyming, including *"Blegburn Bill at Preston Gill"*, and *"Friends are few when fooak are poor"*, licensee Billington wrote prose pieces in the *"Blackburn Standard"*, and two years before his death he penned verses about the town's writers - *"Where are the Blackburn Poets Gone?"* On his death, poets from all over Lancashire penned lines in his praise.

If ever a man wrote a grand poem in praise of his home town, it was Billington when he penned *"Blackburn to the Fore."* Amongst the rousing stanzas is one, much quoted, which is particularly apt for inclusion here:-

In Education, Blackburn claims
To stand on higher ground.
In authorship, to more than rival
Many towns around.

A mate of Billington's was John Thomas Baron (born 1856 in Chapel Street, died 1911) who wrote under the pen-name of *"Jack o'Ann's"*. In 1906 Baron contributed his one thousandth poem to the *"Blackburn Times"*. It was estimated, and cannot be doubted, that those thousand poems contained every known Lancashire dialect word. The first of them was amongst his best - *"A Comfortable Smook"*. One with very local flavour was *"Blackburn Easter Fair"*.

Jack's brother, or one of them, was Joseph Baron (born 1859 at Rishton, died 1924) who wrote as *"Tum o'Dick o'Bob's"* and worked on several Lancashire newspapers in Blackburn and Blackpool. Love of dialect drove him to compile *"The Blegburn Dickshonary"* and *"A Lancashire Dickshonary"* which were light-hearted explanations of dialect words. Confirming that Blackburnians of old used *"dud"* as a past particle instead of *"did"*, he wrote a delightful 5-verse piece called *"He olez dud his nook"*. A craftsmen word-smith, Joseph also wrote plays, one of which ran for some time at the New Sadler's Wells Theatre in London. Their brother William had fewer associations with Blackburn, and although born in Blackpool in 1865 and associated with Rochdale, it was from Blackburn that he was educated and worked for many years, contributing, as *"Bill o' Jack's"* to the *"Blackburn Standard"*. Hull rightly called him *"a poet of the people"*. In 1888 he published in Blackburn his book *"Bits o'Broad Lancashire"*.

A leader of those Lancashire poets who works, smells and tastes of the moorlands is Henry Yates, born on the Lancashire/Yorkshire border at Summit near Littleborough in 1841 where his father was building the Summit railway tunnel. Coming to Blackburn as a seven-year old lad, he attended Nova Scotia School. At night school, the man who became known as *"The Bard of Islington"* began to write pieces for the *"Blackburn Weekly Times"*. He wove cloth for a living and words for pleasure, using the pen-names *"Tansy Tuft"* and *"Giles Catchup"*. I specially like *"Owd Peter"* and the magnificent *"A Lancashire Mon"*.

Aw wer bred amung th' hills, but Aw'm Lanky,
   Ther's no hauf an' hauf abeawt me;
It's deawn i' mi gronny's owd Bible—
   Booath sides of a long pedigree;
Aw've no need to simper an' sidle,
   Nor finnicky airs to put on;
Aw belong to th' owd Palatine Ceawnty—
   Aw'm a streytforrad, Lancashire mon!

Aw con croodle a tune they wer singin'
   When watchfires were blazin' on th' hills,
When t' Ceawnty men buckled ther belts on,
   An' dames wore ther curls an' ther frills;
Aw've a kistful o' heirlooms i' th' kitchen;
   An' Aw've plushes o' aw maks to don;
Aw'm conceited to think 'at Aw'm English,
   But Aw'm preawd Aw'm a Lancashire mon!

Aw've a bak'-stooane, a brack-breyd, an' thible;
   Aw've a breydflake for oatcakes an' o;
Ther's mi deetin' brush, too, an' mi drier,
   An' a warmin' pon hung upo' th' wo;
Ther's mi loom-stocks an' o, up i' th' corner,
   As Aw'll keep till Aw dee, if Aw con,
For they're nicer than t' new-fangled fashion,
   To an owd-fashioned, Lancashire mon!

We play nooan if owt's to be mended:
   We're i' th' vanguard if owt's to be won;
We parcel aw t' werk eawt for t' nations,
   Ere t' world wakkens up to wod's done.
There may be a shire 'at is broader,
   But ther's nobbut one Ceawnty—just one,
'An t' King is a Duke on—that's Lanky,
   An' ther's nowt licks a Lancashire mon!

Henry Yates died in 1906. Gone but not forgotten.

"The Bard of Ribblesdale" was the name given to and adopted by Richard Dugdale (born 1790 (?) died 1875). He was a big, strapping chap, known to put an end to pub brawling. He had been a soldier. He taught himself the trade of engraver, and when forty years old had the reputation of *"best in Lancashire"*. When

147

approaching eighty years old, he could still engrave the Lord's Prayer on a silver threepenny bit. Something of the uneducated orphan comes out in Dugdale's poetry, and something of the *"gentle giant"* so much admired by his contemporaries.

As with Dugdale, the name of Charles Frederick James Nightingale Stott is unknown outside Blackburn. He was born in Australia but arrived in Blackburn before his first birthday in 1862.

"Charlie" died aged 33 in 1894 and lies in Blackburn Cemetery. He deserves recognition in this over-view of Blackburn writers if only for his two poems in praise of *"t'Rovers an' th'Olympic"*.

COMMEMORATION POEM
Addressed to the
Blackburn Rovers' Football Team
April 4th, 1885

Yet once again and we the victors greet—
The Blackburn Rovers' Football Team, the pride
Of Lancashire; the trusted, tested, tried;
The greatest English Team, full firm and fleet
On every football ground, in play, on feet.
Hurrah! Hurrah! Hurrah! the nation's prize*
Reclines once more'neath Blackburn's Easter skies,
Won by her sons of toil, her own *elite*.
Yet once again, the Scottish "Queens", well known
Around, have yielded to the Crimson Rose,
Jus gladii o'er the finest Thistle blown,
The power to hold—O may it ne'er have flown!—
The Challenge Cup, upon the which we close
With bursts of joy in voice, in verse in prose.

*The English Association Challenge Cup was won by the B.R.F.C. for the third time in 1886.

OUR FOOTBALL TEAMS
(Dedicated to the Teams of Blackburn: viz., the Blackburn Rovers and the Blackburn Olympic)

EACH Saturday when days are cold
  And warmer weather fleeting,
Our football teams turn out to give
  Their *"visitors"* a beating.

At Leamington, to widespread fame,
  They dread the "Blackburn Rover";
Or up above the Shire's Brow,
  The "'Lympic" throws them over.

148

To these the "Wand'rer" struck his flag,
    And "Eton" went a-weeping,
Whilst England gave her Challenge Cup
    To Captain Hunter's keeping.

In crowded fields, the lusty cheer,
    From throats nigh choked with cotton,
Proclaims the fact in far-off streets:
    "A goal! a goal! well gotten."

Then toe to toe; go on, brave "blues",
    Through forest, town and heather;
And Blackburn still with cheerful voice
    Shall hail the globe of leather.

Press on to goal and keep the cups
    Ye both have won so bravely,
And point to all inquiring clubs,
    "Old Wykehamists" and "Staveley".

Now in the final eight ye stand,
    To win or lose the trophy;
So here we'll part till "time" is called,
    Then write another 'strophy.

Not fearing yet, I'll trust ye both
    On any field before ye:
True samples of our Blackburn arms,
    Our "*Arte et Labore.*"

Students of Lancashire poetry - not necessarily of dialect verse - will be familiar with the name of John Critchley Prince. "*The Reedmaker Poet*" (born at Wigan 1808, died 1866 at Hyde). He didn't spend much time in Blackburn but made a big impression on his contemporaries whilst he was here, sufficient for inclusion in George Hull's book of Blackburn poets. In 1858, he composed two hymns for the opening of the Infirmary, one of which was sung by a thousand schoolchildren to the tune "*Warrington*".

Rev. Alexander Balloch Grosart is mentioned elsewhere, as is William Westall and the first lady to be mentioned so far, Dorothy Whipple.

A lady poet, Ellen Ling, came to Feniscowles in 1875 and wrote prolifically. She had her work published in book form as well as in the local papers. She wrote one poem in praise of another

149

much-revered Blackburn lady, Mrs Lewis, the Temperance worker, who is referred to elsewhere in this book.

IN MEMORIAM: MRS LEWIS

Servant of God, and friend of erring man—
How nobly hast thou lived the allotted span;
Whole-heartedly hast tracked the drink-fiend down,
And brought unnumbered blessings to our town.

How many homes have been reclaimed by thee;
How many parents snatched from misery;
How many a youth and girl by drink depraved,
By thy kind ministrations have been saved?

How many little ones of tender years
Have looked to thee to dry their falling tears;
How many lips have learned to tell thy fame
And pour their blessings on thine honoured name?

God grant that generations yet may see
Thy works of love and grace to follow thee;
And be thy name remembered to the end:
The "Queen of Temperance" and the "Drunkard's Friend".

Few Members of Parliament achieve literary recognition, but John Morley did. However, it has to be said that he wasn't a creative writer, rather a researcher and an opinionated one. Viscout Morley of Blackburn was born in the town in 1838 and died in London in 1923. Before being a politician he had been a journalist who rose to edit The Pall Mall Gazette. His biographies of Gladstone, Oliver Cromwell and Richard Cobden are standard works.

In more recent times, the name comes to the fore of Alice Miller (nee Bass) *"one of Lancashire's jewels"* who died aged 78 years in 1971. She wrote her first poetry at eight years of age, her first play a year later. She contributed to the local papers and her verses were used in Christmas cards sent by the Royal family. Of her local poems, my favourites are her pair on Blackburn's own Kathleen Ferrier:-

KATHLEEN FERRIER (1)
(1912-1953)

Like some bright bird
Which flutes from spring to autumn;
Soul-true your perfect song held the listening air!
Pure and intense, intense:
And gravely beneficial:
Sweet voice of England, so finely deep and rare!

150

As you have linked
Our hearts and minds to music:
Captured a broken world, and made men whole again:
Fingered, vibrated,
Chords of love, time-dormant:
So shall we cherish you, freed from shackled pain!

NORTHERN LASSIE (2)
I know a Northern lassie
Who sang a Pennine air:
Who, rosy-lipped and proud-lipped,
Made Lancashire more fair!

I heard a Northern lassie
Make tidal waves her song:
And give her heart's full loving
To Lancashire more strong!

I found a Northern lassie
Within my heart, and O
On every ship and dream-star
Her lovely voice will go!

Margaret Munro came to Blackburn as a schoolgirl from her native North Wales. She wrote her first poem in 1894 and won a prize with it. Using her pen-name *"Gilbert Gillespie"*, she achieved some regional significance as a poet. She was a friend of her contemporary Ellen Ling as well as being held in high regard by Blackburn's literary circle. She was a dressmaker.

We have now reached some living writers - the poets are behind us. Firstly, a lady *"Blackburn born and bred"*, Marie Joseph is one of the country's top novelists. She sets her tales in the Blackburn of her younger days. To date, there have been fourteen books, ten of which made the Best Seller list. Marie was struck with arthritis when 25 years old. By the age of forty, she couldn't hold a pen, but starting to use a typewriter turned Marie into a short story writer. She hasn't looked back. Her autobiography *"One Step at a Time"* tells that story, but her appeal to readers is through her translating memories into fiction. Highly recommended for Blackburn readers wanting to find the town as it was is her *"Maggie Craig"* (Century Fiction). Marie's mother died giving her birth, leaving her in the care of her grandmother and aunts, weavers in 1930's Blackburn. Read also her *"Gemini Girls"* and *"Footsteps in the Park"*. Arrow

151

Books recently published The Marie Joseph Omnibus.

Stephen Gallagher, born in Salford in 1954, came to live in Blackburn in the early 1980's. He was described by author James Herbert as being *"in the top league of new-generation chiller writers"*. He describes himself as *"an unremarkable sod who's never been a lumberjack or a bodyguard and who's never shot anybody even as an accident"*. Leaving university with honours in English and Drama, Stephen worked for Granada TV and the BBC. He concentrated on drama serials and radio plays, with episodes of *"Dr. Who"* thrown in for good measure. Publishers Hodder & Stoughton have to date published seven of his books. Readers will easily recognise Blackburn in his novel *"Down River"*, although the town is magnified to the size of Manchester. Most easily recognisable is the Northgate Police Station. In his other stories can be spotted the M6, Charnock Richard Service Station, a moorland village bearing a striking resemblance to Abbey Village, Morecambe Bay, Silverdale and Sunderland Point. His tale *"The Drain'* tells of three lads entering the town's park at night, walking along its broad walkways, entering the drained ornamental lake, finding some wartime unexploded ammunition. It HAS to be Corporation Park.

There's a telling passage in the early pages of *"The Drain"*. It reads:

I went back and took a look at the park again a couple of years ago. The gateway's still there, a big triple archway of sandstone in the Victorian style, but these days it doesn't seem quite so monumental as it did then. There's a carved plaque above the middle entrance to commemorate the fact that the ornamental fountains were presented by the mayor of the borough in 1857. The gates lead through onto a broad central walkway of dull red tarmac, powdered along its edges by fallen debris from the overhanging tree branches. The walkway climbs gently into the heart of the parkland."

Joyce Bentley has lived in Blackburn and Darwen since the early 1960's. She is a much published writer of novels and biographies. Many of her novels have a Manchester setting, as that is where she grew up. However, perhaps Joyce's main contribution to the Blackburn literary scene is through the vast amount of work she has done in teaching creative writing to many who have gone on to establish themselves as writers and had a great deal of pleasure out of her enthusiasm. Amongst her biographies is one on Oscar Wilde's wife called *"The Importance of Being Constance"*. That's what I call clever.

It's good to know that the most-borrowed books in Blackburn

Library are by a Blackburn writer. Josephine Cox has written, to date, twelve books, all set in her native town. They are fictional with that strong vein of home-spun truth which Blackburnians can recognise, though ranging in period from 1850 to the 1970's. Corporation Park features in most of them, as does the Navigation Inn, Mill Hill. This isn't surprising when Josephine, on one of her frequent visits to Blackburn to visit friends and relatives, admits to spending hours in the park, dreaming under a willow tree.

Born in the early days of the war in Derwent Street as Josephine Brindle, one of ten children to a mother working in a mill and a father working as a Corporation groundsman, she attended St Anne's School, and recalls going on Ragged School trips to the seaside. When her parents split up, Josephine went South with her mother at the age of 14 years. She soon found romance and love, and married when sixteen. That marriage flourishes yet.

Look out for Blackburn characters you will recognise in her books. *"Emma Grady"* has cropped up in three of them in an area recognisable as Montague Street and Preston New Road.

Josephine's books are not popular in Blackburn alone. She is a *"top-ten"* fiction writer. Her books have been translated into Italian and Polish, and she is asked questions about her native town by Australian readers. If you see a coachload of people near the Navigation Inn, they'll be seeking out Josephine Cox's Blackburn.

Her 12 books are entitled *"Alley Warden", "Angels Cry Sometimes", "Don't Cry Alone", "Her Father's Sins", "Jessica's Girl", "Let Loose the Tigers", "Nobody's Darling", "Outcast", "Scarlet", "Take This Woman", "Vagabonds", "Whistledown Woman".* She also writes books in a different style and setting as *"Jane Brindle".*

Dorothy Whipple
Betty Smith

I have often felt, that, in comparison with Blackburn's famous daughter Kathleen Ferrier, Dorothy Whipple's skill, popularity and fame have never been truly acknowledged by her native town. I was first introduced to the novels of Dorothy Whipple by my mother, who was an absolute devotee of all that Dorothy ever wrote. Having been reared on a diet of Enid Blyton, then graduating to Ursula Bloom, and Angela Thirkell, I came to read Dorothy Whipple's writings, as probably my first exploration into the world of adult literature. My mother was almost a contemporary of Dorothy, and related how she used to see Dorothy, auburn-haired and very straight-backed, walking down Preston New Road, on her way to work as Secretary to the Director of Education. Living in the same Billinge district as the Stirrup family, I think I regarded her almost as a family friend! I used to walk past the various houses that she had lived in with a sense of awe, almost as though I were on Holy Ground!

Dorothy Stirrup, to call her by her maiden name, was born in Edgeware Road, Blackburn, on February 26th 1893. She was the second child of Walter and Ada Stirrup and her father was an architect.

Dorothy Whipple's autobiography is entitled *"The Other Day"*. In this book she describes her early childhood in Blackburn, and many of the places are easily recognisable, even from this distance in time. She describes *"The Tank"* off Revidge Road.

"From the top of the hill, just above our house you could look down on the one hand, at the town, spiked with smoking mill chimneys, and on the other had, over thirty miles of fields and woods rolling without interruption to the sea.

On a clear day Blackpool Tower showed like a skeleton in the sky, with the wheel a little "O" beside it. In those days, people simpler than they are now, made family excursions in the evenings to the top of the Tank, an unlovely reservoir, to catch a glimpse of this same sea. The air that blew in at the windows of my first home came from the sea. They said you could taste the salt on your lips when there was a carrying wind. It was fresh, keen air, but it was often wet. Alas, very often wet. In fact to be fully equipped for life in my native town you ought to be born in a mackintosh and umbrella."

She describes the walks the family took with their maid to the Yellow Hills, between the Walls, which was the walk along what is now Under Billinge Lane, and visits to Corporation Park, where she describes the Conservatory, the old Band Stand, which stood near West Park Road, opposite Q.E.G.S. She also says at one point to her brothers, when they are trying to decide where to go on their walk, *"Let's go to the Park, and stand on that part near the Lake, where it feels as if you are sailing!"* I well remember that particular spot, where a large iron drainage cover jutted out into the Lake, and you felt isolated and cut off, when you stood there!

Research by my friend, Barbara Riding, has shown that the first school she attended was in Shear Bank Road, and was run by two sisters, the Misses Barretts, Doorthy Whipple is an expert at final comments, which just describe the situation or the atmosphere. Perhaps just a single sentence, and in the passage where Dorothy describes the clothes and the habits of her first experience of teachers, she describes how she sat very close to the teacher, so close that *"When she rumbled abdominally, I listened with awe!!!"*

From this school, Dorothy transferred to the High School. This was not a very happy period in her life. Her developing literary talent was not recognised, and she later transferred to The Convent. We can identify the position of the Convent on Whalley Old Road, from her description.

"Once the Convent had been the country mansion of an old Lancashire family, but little by little the tide of mills, streets, houses and shops had crept over the fields, flowed round the house and far out beyond. The Convent with its great enclosed garden made a green isle in a sea of slate waves, over which rode the pounding vessels of industry, the cotton mills."

Dorothy's parents sent her and her brothers to a Bible Class which was held above a solicitor's office in what is easily recognisable as Richmond Terrace. She describes it so:

"We arrived at length in the deserted Terrace, and were briefly heartened by the sight of our father's name on his office windows."

Dorothy writes a most graphic description of the *"Shrimp Women"* on Blackburn Market,

"The shrimp-women came from Southport to sit in the Market Place on Wednesday and Saturday. These women wore voluminous

155

*print skirts and sprigged cotton sun-bonnets all the year round, with
the addition of triangular woollen shawls in the Winter. As far as I
can remember they all had club feet. I thought perhaps you got club
feet from catching shrimps. I thought it was what would now be
called a vocational defect, but I suppose it was merely coincidence.*

*The shrimp-women sat in the open cobbled space, looking cheerful
and clean in starched print and highly polished club boots. At their
feet, in shallow baskets covered with checked cloths, lay the tender
pink crescents of their famous pinked shrimps."*

*"The Market-House was such a complete place to me. You could
live there, I thought, and with all your wants supplied. In the middle
were stalls of books, music and toys, and round the sides were places
like one-roomed houses where you could go and eat tea-cake or roast
pork beside a blazing fire, while a comfortable woman in an apron
tied on over her shawl, stood outside and invited others in."*

*"'Pork's nice today,' they would remark, 'Come in and have a
plate of pork.' I longed to take them at their word, but no one would
let me."*

Dorothy eventually married Henry Whipple, who was the
Director of Education for Blackburn from 1908-1924. He was
twenty-six years older than her. Dorothy's first book, *"Young
Anne"* was published in 1924. A best-seller *"They were Sisters"*
was made into a film, and other book, *"Because of the Lockwoods"*
was made into a radio play. The titles of her other books are
*"Someone at a Distance", "The Priory", "They knew Mr. Knight",
"Every Good Deed", "Greenbanks",* and *"High Wages".*

Dorothy and Henry Whipple had a very happy marriage in spite
of the difference in their ages. In 1925, they moved to Nottingham,
and she describes their life there in the second volume of her
autobiography, called *"Random Commentary".* This book is
compiled from Note Book and Diary jottings, and covers the period
from 1925-1945. In this book we see Dorothy emerging as an
author. She describes the process by which her books were
published, and how she suffers the anguish of rejection, and the
excitement of success. J.B. Priestley became a very close friend of
Henry and Dorothy, and he described Dorothy Whipple as *"the
Jane Austen of the Twentieth Century".*

Dorothy's description of a train journey from Nottingham to
Blackburn is evocative of a by-gone age.

*"I set off for Blackburn, by train, on a dreadful snowy day. At
Manchester Victoria, I was told I had an hour to wait for the
Blackburn train, I knew I was 'home' the moment I alighted from*

the Nottingham train. 'Here love,' said the porter. 'Give me your case, You'd better go and get a cup of tea. I'll come and fetch you when t' train's due. You sit in't refreshment room as long as possible and keep warm!' .... Nowhere but in Lancashire, I think, does a porter speak to you, like that!"

After the death of her husband in 1958, Dorothy returned to live in Blackburn. She lived in Whinfield Place, on Preston New Road, just below Billinge End. Her life-long friend, May Whittaker and Dorothy, picked up their friendship once more, and for the rest of Dorothy's life, met for tea every Saturday afternoon. Her friend describes Dorothy thus, *"She was a highly intelligent and very gifted woman, very kind and always full of sympathy towards people with problems. She had a tremendous devotion to animals, and her own three cats she had found as strays. She loved children also, and would treat anybody's children as though they were her own."*

Dorothy Whipple died in September 1966. A proud Lancastrian, and a person in whom her native town can also take much pride.

William (Bury) Westall 1834-1903

Eddie Cass

William Westall is one of those now forgotten minor nineteenth century novelists who tried to mediate the working conditions of *'cotton Lancashire'* to a wider, national readership. This readership was drawn, in part, from the ranks of the patrons of Mudie's Circulating Library. In addition, however, Westall had a significant following among the reader's of the serials which were an important feature in the provincial newspapers of the late Victorian and Edwardian periods. Mrs Gaskell, Disraeli and Dickens all wrote about Manchester and Lancashire for an earlier generation of readers. They continue to be read and studied for their *'condition of England'* novels. Westall is among a large group of writers who continued the tradition of writing about Lancashire after the middle of the nineteenth century by which time the national interest in the cotton towns had abated. It is a group of writers which, unfortunately, now only has an interest for students of minor Victorian and Edwardian writers or of novels about Lancashire.

William Bury Westall was born at White Ash, Church, near Blackburn on 7th February 1834. He was the eldest son of John, a cotton spinner of White Ash and Ann, daughter of James Bury Entwistle. Westall was educated in Liverpool at the High School. It was while he was at school that Westall first earned money through his ability to tell stories. He used to relate how his gifts for story-telling were in great demand. It was the custom for one of the boys to tell stories for the benefit of his fellows in the dormitory once the lights were out. William was known to have a splendid memory for tales and could remember the plot of any story he had once read. He was a favourite with his school-fellows and was called upon so often that he once refused to continue with his tales. His listeners thereupon had a collection and raised some three shillings and sixpence, a sum sufficient to induce Westall to resume the narrative. On leaving school, Westall went to work in his father's cotton-spinning business. However, at the age of 36, he changed careers. He retired from the family business, went to live abroad and became a journalist. He started off by sending articles to *The Times* and *The Spectator* but on moving to Geneva in 1874 he became a foreign correspondent. In addition, he became part owner and editor of *The Swiss Times*. He used his experiences at this time as the basis of a novel *Her Two Millions* (published in 1897) which depicts with humour the conditions of Anglo-continental journalism in Geneva at a time when the city was also home to a number of exiled Russian revolutionaries. These expatriates included Prince Kropotkin with whom Westall became aquainted. It was here that Westall also got to know Sergei Mikhailowitch Kravchinsky who subsequently moved to London at Westall's suggestion. The two men later collaborated on translations of contemporary Russian literature. Westall's first book was similarly reflective of his travel experiences; *Tales and Traditions of Saxony and Lusatia* was published in 1877. Despite these, perhaps somewhat erudite, pieces of work, Westall's success as a writer was based on his first novel *The Old Factory*. He had submitted this novel to W.F. Tillotson of Bolton about 1880. At that time, Tillotson was the proprietor of the largest and best known provincial fiction bureau. The novel was accepted by the bureau for syndication in their newspapers.

The Old Factory. A Lancashire Story was orginally published in book-form by Tinsley's in 1881 as a three-decker (i.e. 3 volumes), the format which was so much in demand from the circulating libraries for their largely middle class readership. In addition to appearing as a three-decker, the novel later appeared in several one volume editions. *The Old Factory* tells the story of the Blackthorne family, starting with Adam Blackthorne's employment as a putter out for a Manchester cotton merchant following the death of his father. Blackthorne, by dint of that diligence which was expected of up and coming manufacturers, makes his way in the world. It is the involvement of his son with a less than satisfactory woman by the name of Lydia Fell which provides a setback in what should otherwise have been an unblemished rise in the standing of the Blackthorne family and its inter-marriage with the Basel family, neighbours and business connections of Adam Blackthorne. The story is set against the background of the rise and development of the Lancashire cotton industry from the early hand-loom weaving days to steam driven weaving and spinning factories. The setting is a Lancashire mill community between Blackburn ('*Redburn*') and Accrington ('*Orrington*') before the larger mill towns had come to dominate the industry. Inevitably, there are conflicts between the autocratic Adam Blackthorne and his workers but in the end, as one might expect, Frank Blackthorne exhibits the qualities of a concerned employer, anxious to see the family's employees well looked after. Just as the relationships between masters and men are satisfactorily settled then so are the marriage arrangements between the two Blackthorne children and the two Basel children. What the novel does do is to explain to a readership not necessarily familiar with Lancashire and its textile industry, what this new Lancashire was about. Readers of three-deckers might have heard of the textile industry of Lancashire, but what Westall was doing - in addition to telling a very popular story - was conveying to his readers some idea of what life was like in those often remote mill communities. The novel was certainly successful for it ran into several editions. It was also extensively serialised in Lancashire newspapers.

Having started off his travels in Europe, Westall also visited North and South America and the West Indies. He was not averse to using his experiences in these countries in order to provide a background for his novels. *Red Ryvington*, for example, has adventures set in the Rhone Valley, in Switzerland and in Russia where Randle Ryvington meets Sergius Kalongia who becomes a lifelong friend! Echoes of Westall's own life with the expatriate Russians. In that part of the novel set in England, Preston is *'Ribbleton'*, Blackburn is *'Whitebrook'* and Feniscowles becomes *'Deepdene'*. Local people who find a place in the novel include Thomas Ainsworth, a solicitor, appears as *'Thomas Pleasington'* and the artisan poet William Billington is renamed *'William Bentley'*. Again, there is much in this Lancashire part which is informative about local factory life in a pattern which is familiar Westall - local settings juxtaposed with foreign travel and adventures which very much reflected the author's own life.

After his period of travel and living overseas, Westall returned to England and settled in Worthing, Sussex. In 1903 he let his house, *'Rydal'*, in Wordsworth Road and went for a six week holiday to Heathfield, Sussex where he died on 9th September.

T.P. O'Connor, Westall's friend wrote of him,

"He was a thorough-paced Lancashire man - bustling and keen when business was in the air, and straight as a rush. Cosmopolitan as the fates tried to render him, he always regarded his native county as the hub of the universe. He was a Blackburn man ..."

Westall was buried at Heathfield. He was married twice, the first time on 13th March 1855 to Ellen Anne Wood, the second daughter of Christopher Wood of Silverdale, Lancashire. They had two sons and one daughter. On 2nd August 1863 he married Ellen's elder sister Alicia and they had two sons and two daughters.

Westall's best known novels included *Larry Lohengrin*, (1879), (also published as *John Brown and Larry Lohengrin*, (1889), *The Old Factory*, (1881), *Red Ryvington*, (1882), *Ralph Norbreck's Trust* (1885), *The Phantom City*, *(1886)*, *A Fair Crusader*, (1888), *Roy of Roy's Court*, (1892), *The Witch's Curse*, (1893), *As a Man Sows*, (1894), *Sons of Belial*, *(1895)*, *With The Red Eagle*, (1897), *Her Two Millions*, (1897), *Don or Devil*, (1901), *The Old Bank*, (1902).

The Reverend Alexander Grosart

Hilton Kelliher

How many people in Blackburn recognise the name of Alexander Balloch Grosart (1827-1899)? In the annals of the town he has, as a Scot, taken second place to the Hornbys, Harrisons, Pilkingtons, Thwaites and Duttons, all home-bred men. In the larger world his younger contemporary John, Viscount Morley of Blackburn (1838-1923) - radical, journalist, biographer, and Cabinet minister - made the greater mark.

Yet Grosart deserves to be remembered with honour. It is not so much that for almost a quarter of a century he served as minister of St. George's United Presbyterian Church in Preston New Road. His main claim to fame lies in the contribution that he made to the study of English literature. In an age that was fascinated by everything Elizabethan, Grosart became its most productive editor of English renaissance texts. For this he is still remembered in places of learning all over the English-speaking world.

Between 1868 and 1892, the period of his ministry, an endless stream of pioneering editions of Tudor and Stuart poets issued from his study.. In all, his published volumes numbered more than three hundred. Such a vast and scholarly output, leavened by wide reading, was no mean achievement for a busy Victorian clergyman in a central Lancashire cotton town.

In addition, along with many practical tracts of religion and a large number of hymns, Grosart was a tireless contributor to periodicals. He wrote many articles for the ninth edition of the *Encylopaedia Britannica*. In 1887 his own University of Edinburgh bestowed on him the Doctorate of Letters: Aberdeen made him a Doctor of Divinity.

Grosart was born in Stirling in 1835, the son of a builder and contractor, and early in life acquired the habit of voracious reading. At Edinburgh University his Professors were Sir William Hamilton and John Wilson (*'Christopher North'*, the essayist). Both had been friends of Wordsworth; and it was perhaps owing to their example that in later life Grosart produced the first collected edition of the poet's prose works (1876).

In October 1856, following his ordination, he took charge of the Presbyterian chapel at Kinross, where he gained repute as preacher, a writer of religious manuals and an antiquary. While there he married the daughter of a Dublin J.P. In 1865 he accepted a call to the new congregation of Princes Park, Liverpool, transferring on 4 March 1868 to Mount Street Presbyterian Church in Blackburn.

As related by the local historian W.A. Abrams, the history of the Blackburn congregation began about 1810, when a party of seceders from the Chapel Street Independent Congregation founded a new sect on Presbyterian principles, in connection with the Burgher Seceders from the Church of Scotland. They built a chapel in Mount Street, and eventually formed links with the Lancashire Presbytery of the United Presbyterian Church.

Their success was such that Mount Street became too small for them, and in 1865, a new place of worship was begun in Preston New Road. Dedicated to St. George, it was designed in the style known as early decorated, with a spire one hundred and twenty-six feet in height. It was completed at a cost of £9,100 and opened on 18 June 1868.

Grosart thus took over a brand new church. During his ministry membership of the Blackburn congregation almost tripled. In November 1892 ill health forced him to resign, and he retired to Dublin where he died on 16 March 1899, after a long and painful illness. In the now demolished St. George's he was commemorated by a tablet that paid tribute to him as *"A learned divine. An eloquent preacher'*.

In his twenty-four years in Blackburn Grosart occupied a succession of houses, often given after his signature in the prefaces to his books.

1869   15 St. Alban's Place.
1873   55 Preston New Road (south side)
1874   *'Park View'*
1879   5 February *'Brooklyn House'*
1881-1887   93 Preston New Road (south side)
1887-1888   *'Brooklyn House'*
1889-1890   70 Preston New Road (north side)

Of these nos. 55 and 70 Preston New Road are still standing: no. 93 has been rebuilt.

Grosart's major literary projects began in the very year of his arrival in Blackburn. The first was a series of editions to which he gave the name of the *"Fuller's Worthies Library"*, after Thomas

Fuller, author of the brief biographies of famous men entitled *Worthies of England* (1662). It was mostly printed, between 1868 and 1876, by Charles Tiplady whose bookshop and printing-house stood on the north side of Church Street, near Salford Bridge. (Tiplady himself was the subject of a memoir in Abram's *Blackburn Characters*.)

The series ran to thirty-nine volumes, and included editions of poems by Fulke Greville, Phinas Fletcher, the Catholic Sir John Beaumont, the Metaphysicals Henry Vaughan and Andrew Marvell, and Thomas Fuller himself. Clearly Grosart's literary tastes were not confined to writers of a nonconformist temper! A supplementary collection entitled *Miscellanies of the Fuller's Worthies Library*, comprising works by other writers of the period, was issued from Tiplady's press in four volumes between 1870 and 1876.

Like all Grosart's literary publications these works were printed privately for subscribers, in editions running only to a hundred, and sometimes to a mere fifty, copies. As a consequence they are nowadays very rarely met with in secondhand and antiquarian bookshops. In recent years many of them have been reissued by reprint-houses in America and Germany.

On their first appearance Grosart's pioneering editions set new standards in the field. Even now, more than one hundred years after they were first published, they still repay careful study. For all the irritating pomposity and antiquarian fussiness of their manner his *'Memorial-introductions'* provided in many cases the first serious attempt at biographies of their subjects. The texts themselves represented a new departure for their time in that they often drew extensively on the evidence of contemporary manuscripts.

When not working, with his customary rapidity, in libraries throughout England he shared his interests with local men of similar tastes. These included William Harrison of Salmesbury Hall, whose name crops up among the subscribers to his works. Harrison's extensive collection of Shakespeariana, put up for sale at Sotheby's in January 1881 following his suicide, included many of Grosart's published works.

His church is gone and his reputation as a minister is forgotten. But it ought still to be a matter of pride to Blackburn folk that the formula *'Alexander B. Grosart ... of St. George's, Blackburn, Lancashire'* appears on the title pages of all his many editions.

The Contributors

This book would not have been published without the essays contributed freely by the following people, whose efforts I greatly appreciate:-

Hilton Kelliher is a Lancashire lad in exile in London. He works at the British Library, formerly the British Museum, on historical and literary manuscripts.

Benita Moore is a librarian interested in *"keeping Lancashire alive"*, which she does by visiting old folk, recording their memories and compiling books around these chats. This aside, she is a talented writer of verse and short stories.

Pauline Hutchinson is an Accrington housewife. She edits the Lancashire Authors' Association magazine, *"The Record"*.

Eddie Cass has researched extensively on Victorian Lancashire working class literature and is working for a PhD degree on the role of Lancashire newspapers in bringing literature into the lives of the working classes.

Betty Smith. Blackburn-born and bred Betty (nee Jones) is a retired teacher married to Gerald. She is a Unitarian minister who enjoys her church work, walking, caravanning, being a grandma and reading (especially Dorothy Whipple).

Alan Duckworth worked for several years in Blackburn Library where his local history interest was encouraged. He is now Local History Librarian in Lancaster. He has recently published a book on Darwen where he lives. He contributed to *"Blackburn & Darwen A Century Ago"*.

Ian Sutton. Ian is Local History and Reference Librarian at Blackburn Library. His contribution to this book goes far beyond the essay on Blackburn's first brewery. His colleagues say he is *"daft on t'Rovers"*.

Nick Howorth. Educated at Q.E.G.S., Nick is a pathologist in a Blackpool hospital but still maintains strong and frequent connections with his home town.

George Worledge has researched extensively the life of his great, great Uncle V.O. Sherwood, whose fine painting on the ceremonial laying of the foundation stone of Blackburn's Cotton Exchange hangs in the entrance hall of the town's Art Gallery. George has translated his ancestor's diary and has visited Russia to meet his relatives.

Rev. Walter Fancutt was born in 1911 into church mouse poverty. He was 14 years old when he signed a *"Lad's Discipleship for God"* form at the Ragged School, and remembers seeing the school's founders. He went for training as a missionary to London when aged 18 years. He worked as a Baptist minister in the South of England since 1934. He has contributed to *"The Baptist Times"* since 1942, and has written many books. He lives with his wife in the Isle of Wight, with part of his heart still in Blackburn.

Alan Pickering lives and works in Blackburn as a fire engineer. He is an avid researcher and collector of local history material, and author of a book on New Row. His ambitions include further writing on Livesey and Tockholes.

Rev. Chris Damp is a Congregational minister in a London church. He regards himself as *"a Leyland lad"* with an interest in church history. He worked for some months in Blackburn's Salvation Army hostel about 1984.

Eddie Conway worked in Blackburn 1975-79 for the Workers' Educational Association, and through his work with the Asian community became interested in previous immigrants to the town. He contributed an extended study of the Blackburn Jewish community to a 1977 Conference on Victorian Provincial Communities. He now lives in Liverpool.

Stanley Miller is the son of one of Blackburn's finest historians, George. Now retired from a lifetime spent in Blackburn Library, where, as Local History Librarian his equal is unlikely to be met again, he keeps up his interest in the town's past with active membership of the Local History Society. My debt of gratitude to Stanley is immense.

Gerry Wolstenholme is a senior Civil Servant with a passion for cricket at all levels. He writes, broadcasts ball-for-ball, contributes to several magazines, is the author of one book, collects cricketabilia and lectures on his favourite sport. This love affair isn't secret - his wife Linda is as cricket-daft as he is.

Harry Berry has been a Rovers supporter since he was eight years old (he is now 48 years) forty years ago. He is financial director to one of Blackburn's largest employers, but still finds time to be a road runner. A prolific author, he has written a history of Blackburn Rovers, a series of four books on different aspects of the

Rovers' past teams as well as one on Preston North End and four others on athletics. If you see someone running past wearing a blue and white shirt and scribbling on a pad - it'll be Harry.

Marc Duckworth has lived in Blackburn most of his life. He's in his 30's, interested in local history and archaeology, which interests have been aroused through his metal detecting activities.

Christine Wilks is a former librarian turned housewife and young mother. She completed a study on Blackburn murders as part of her professional studies whilst working in Blackburn Library.

John Gavan is a retired policeman, living with his wife Sheila at Belthorn. He has an interest in canals, history, tales and ales. He studied the Blackburn Workhouse when undertaking a course *"for something to do"* at Blackburn College.

James A. Marsden is a private landlord with a deep interest in old Blackburn and its buildings. He has frequently contributed information on such matters to the local newspapers.

Graham Chadwick is a former Head of the Harrison Institute. He served on Blackburn Town Council for some time. Graham teaches Creative Writing and has written many poems and short stories. His other interest is in gardening.

Dorothy Ashburn Canham is a retired Blackburn teacher with a great interest in the town's history and physical aspects.

Adrian Lewis came to work in Blackburn in 1971, attracted by the Edward Hart Collection of coins in the musuem. He is Head of Arts & Heritage Services for the town. Already a published author with books on the Civil War in Lancashire and the East Lancashire Regiment amongst others, he is working on a general history of the town and on a biography of *"Monkey"* Hornby.

Andrew Kit is just 23 years old, a newly qualified Industrial designer. He submitted a dissertation on *"Photography in Victorian & Edwardian Blackburn"* towards his degree. He shares with Justine Cotton the distinction of being the youngest contributor.

Ken Fields is a retired (early) engineer with a life-long love of walking and of books. He is a freelance writer on countryside matters and lives at Egerton.

Helen Wood lives near Bury. she has a great interest in Victorian women writers and fashion, contributing to learned journals on these subjects. Her other interests are in theatre and music.

Michael Herschell lived in Blackburn for nearly five years, working as a primary school teacher and freelance writer. He now lives in Shropshire and is actively pursuing his collecting of information on

British cemeteries, as he hopes to write a book on the subject. He spends much time in digging - gardens, not graves.

Justine Cotton shares with Andrew Kit the distinction of being the youngest contributor to this book. Formerly a pupil at St. Mary's College, she studied for her Social History Degree at Exeter University, and prepared a study on Blackburn's Weavers for it. A Langho girl, she now lives and works in London in accountancy.

Arthur Fisher came to Blackburn *"with his job"* in 1983 and soon became interested in the town's past. Currently working on a study of Blackburn's Public Health, he was a founder member, now Chairman, of the Blackburn Local History Society.